DE SHAZER

The Doolittle Raider

Who Turned Missionary

No Longer Enemies

Captain Mitsuo Fuchida, leader of the Japanese squadron which bombed Pearl Harbor, talks with DeShazer through whose influence he was brought to Christ. DeShazer shows effects of his 40-day fast in spring of 1950.

On April 18, 1942
. . . DeShazer with others took off the U. S. S. Hornet to bomb and blast Japan. He was captured and tortured in prison for 40 months.

On December 28, 1948
. . . DeShazer returned to Japan as an emissary of good will. He is now the "best known and beloved Christian missionary in Japan."

DE SHAZER

The Doolittle Raider
Who Turned Missionary

By

CHARLES HOYT WATSON

A True and Thrilling Story of How the Practical
Demonstration of the Law of Love is Bring-
ing International Understanding and the
Spirit of Christ to Japan

THE LIGHT AND LIFE PRESS
WINONA LAKE, INDIANA

First printing, November, 1950—5,000
Second printing, January, 1951—10,000
Third printing, December, 1951—5,000
Fourth printing, February, 1952—5,000
Fifth printing, May, 1952, 10,000

DEDICATED

*To the memory of my godly parents,
the Reverend and Mrs. Isaac Newton Watson*

PREFACE

Soon after Jacob DeShazer returned to Japan as a Christian missionary there was a great demand for a book concerning his conversion. In order to comply with that request and also to reach additional thousands with the Gospel message, Mr. DeShazer wrote and published in Japanese an account of his life. This autobiography containing much personal testimony, sincere exhortation, and Scripture exposition as well as his prison experiences is having wide circulation throughout Japan.

Much use has been made of this autobiography in preparing this book. Most of the quotations from DeShazer appearing herein were taken from the English version of this Japanese publication.

The author, however, has spared no effort in gathering additional pertinent material from other sources. These include Army Personnel Records, Documents from the post-war Allied War Trials Court, news dispatches, war reports, private correspondence with DeShazer's comrades in prison, particularly with Lieutenant (now Captain) C. J. Nielson, many interviews and much correspondence with DeShazer and others.

The author is indebted especially to the International News Service, the Associated Press, the Wide World Photos, and several individuals for permission to use their pictures. He wishes to express thanks also for valuable help and encouragement received from Dr. Don R. Falkenberg, President of the Bible Meditation League; Colonel Cyril D. Hill of the U. S. Army; the Reverend Philip E. Armstrong of the Far Eastern Gospel Crusade,

Guideposts Associates, Inc.; the Reverend Bob Pierce of the Youth for Christ International; Dr. B. H. Pearson of the Oriental Missionary Society; Mr. Lowell Thomas, Radio News-Commentator; Mr. Russell T. Hitt of the *Christian Life Magazine;* Dr. Byron S. Lamson, General Missionary Secretary of the Free Methodist Church; Mr. B. H. Gaddis of the Light and Life Press; Miss C. May Marston, who critically read portions of the manuscript, and other members of the faculty of Seattle Pacific College, and numerous others whose assistance has been equally real. In particular should be mentioned the patience and criticisms of his wife, Elsie, who has been gracious enough to listen to or review the various versions of the book as it became crystallized in its present form.

CHARLES HOYT WATSON

Seattle Pacific College
Seattle, Washington
August 1, 1950

CONTENTS

LIST OF ILLUSTRATIONS

FOREWORD

Jacob DeShazer is "a man sent from God." You have here the story of an ordinary man, wholly dedicated to the mission of bringing a lost world to Christ. It is a story of "a bad man made good by the power of Christ."

Here is a man, untaught and untutored in Biblical theology. With a copy of the Bible available to him for a limited time, in his solitary confinement at a Japanese prison camp, he experiences the great illumination. The light that was in the face of Jesus Christ shines into his desperate, sinful, despairing heart.

But read his story! Here is Christian love "made flesh," living in a Japanese prison. A war prisoner, victim of brutal treatment, responds with love and kindness. He turns the other cheek, loves his enemies, and prays for those who hate and persecute! This is NEWS! The modern cynic says, "Nobody ever lives this way. This is for theological discussion, but not for Main Street. It exists in Heaven, but not here!"

Jacob DeShazer's life gives the lie to all such temporizing. Such a change is unexplainable in human terms. The bombardier, with a heart of hate, is changed! Here is miracle—hate turned to love—living in this world! But there is more. DeShazer finds the only basis for world peace. It is a realistic approach. What Christ can do for DeShazer, He can do for the world. So DeShazer's steps are dogged by newspaper reporters, trying to discover his secret. Crowds gather to hear his simple story. Thousands repent of their sins in his services. The Associated Press estimates the number of converts at 30,000 during his first year in Japan. By his own report, 4,000 confessed and repented of their sins, and gave evidence of changed lives, in one 15-day campaign!

Here is a cool, fresh, invigorating breeze from the Eternal City, to inspire the disillusioned and strengthen the weary. God's in His world, working through DeShazer, changing men and changing the world. This is the power of the Gospel unto salvation, of which we are not ashamed!

None know better than the author what a transformation has taken place in this former Doolittle bombardier. President C. Hoyt Watson of Seattle Pacific College has observed the changes in this earnest Christian student. While studying hard to finish his college course, and prepare for missionary service in Japan, DeShazer, by his life and word, won the esteem of faculty and students. President Watson has given us this forthright version of the DeShazer saga. But this is not all. He describes the religious situation in Japan today and challenges the young people of the Christian colleges in America to enter wholeheartedly into what may prove to be the greatest opportunity for Christianity in all the Christian centuries. This is the book of the year for you. It may change your whole life!

Byron S. Lamson

INTRODUCTION

Early on the morning of December 28, 1948, the world witnessed another startling event in one of the greatest continuing miracles in modern missionary annals.

The International Press had been alerted. Representatives from the Japanese Press were waiting. Photographers were standing by. Military men, civil authorities, religious leaders, old men, young men, women, and children were at the Yokohama dock anxiously awaiting the arrival of a steamship from America.

Why all the excitement? Word had been flashed from America that the Doolittle raider who had turned missionary was to arrive on a ship that very morning.

Little did the populace know the wonderful and miraculous story connected with the modest young man, who was the center of attention as he with his wife and son came down the gang plank. But Ex-Sergeant (now the Reverend) Jacob DeShazer knew. He knew the meaning of a Christian home; he knew how a mother's prayers can follow one; he knew the discouragement of failure, the remorse of sin, the call to daring achievement, the reproach of being captured, the pain of punishment, the meaning of a death sentence—and a thousand other experiences.

But on this December morning, when the sky was overcast and rain was falling, DeShazer, for that is what we shall call him in this narrative, was not thinking of the many things which were in the minds of the news writers. His thoughts reached into the past, but not to recount experiences of pain and suffering. Instead, he was thinking of his debt to Christ for making it possible for him, who nearly seven years before had flown over Japan to kill and destroy, now to return with a message of love and hope.

As he viewed the throng at the dock, his thoughts quickly shifted from the past to the future. Here was Japan, once a great though pagan nation, now a defeated and dis- illusioned people. What poverty, what spiritual hunger! Yes—but *what an opportunity!*

Within a few days he was being called upon to speak to various Japanese groups. Within a few weeks he was speaking many times a day. News of the return to Japan of a man whom the Japanese had tortured in prison for more than three years gripped the popular mind. Churches, schools, factories, clubs, and other organizations were calling for him to come and tell what to them seemed an unbelievable story.

Interest in DeShazer's return to Japan has been world- wide. Seldom has there been a greater demonstration of such interest by all peoples as in this sincere and bona fide application of the principles of Christianity to peace and understanding between nations. Sermons are many and books are plentiful which extol the Golden Rule and the Sermon on the Mount, but to see these principles embodied in an actual, living person was a new kind of news.

Many have been the instances, particularly during a national or world crisis, when individual men have become heroic. Great emergencies, like wars, produce leaders whose names become immortal. Not often, however, does a man reach the heights of public attention and world ap- probation merely by loving his enemies and acting accord- ingly. Herein lies the beauty and interest of the DeShazer narrative. In this regard it appeals to the Christian and the non-Christian alike.

But to the Christian there is far more than beauty and

interest. There is a recognition and an appreciation of the hand of God. The Christian agrees that it has not been chance that the life of DeShazer has moved along as it has.

To indicate something of the love and mercy of God in one young man's life is one purpose of this story. It is not to laud DeShazer, his parents, his college, his church, nor his mission. Rather, it is to honor the Lord and for His glory, to show how God intervened in answering prayer by bringing a rebellious army man to accept Christ as his Lord and Saviour, and also to show how the Lord opened the way for this new convert to give himself so completely into the hands of God that he was able to carry out his prison decision to return to Japan as a messenger of God's love and grace.

Another purpose in publishing this narrative is to assist in further arousing the Christian people of America and the world to the urgency of the present situation in Japan. With the continued development of international thinking in the direction of two opposing ideologies and continued war and rumors of war, particularly in the Orient, it is imperative that intensive action be taken if the Christian way of life is to be adopted by the Japanese. General Mac-Arthur has made a noteworthy call for Bibles and missionaries. DeShazer and others have responded. Many organizations are going to extreme lengths in an effort to accelerate the missionary program.

Japan's doors are open today. How long this will be true is not known. Let the reader, therefore, note the experiences of DeShazer—his conversion, his yielding to the love of God, his decision to express this love to his former enemies, his intensive training for missionary service, his return to Japan and his indefatigable efforts to tell the Japanese people concerning the love of God. As a result

I trust that the reader will likewise be gripped by a personal call to do something about Japan and the Orient.

Still more personal is the desire of the author that every reader of this narrative shall himself be led to a closer walk with God. DeShazer published his own life story in Japanese for the primary purpose of bringing people to Christ. In like manner he shares with the author of this English publication an equal desire that many readers will respond without reserve to the call of God in their own lives.

We shall begin the story as the reader would wish—with DeShazer's childhood and youth.   C. H. W.

Main Street, Madras, Oregon
This was DeShazer's home town throughout his boyhood and youth.

Madras High School
DeShazer graduated here in 1931.

DeShazer Loved Animals
Here he is with armload of pups.

Mother and Son Were Pals
DeShazer and his mother frequently went fishing together on the Deschutes River.

A High School Grad
As DeShazer appeared in his High
School Annual.

Church in Madras
Where, as a boy, DeShazer attended
Sunday school.

CHAPTER I

A PRODUCT OF THE WESTERN FRONTIER

Jacob DeShazer was born in Salem, Oregon, November 15, 1912. His parents were devout Christian people of modest circumstances. His father was a minister-farmer in the Church of God. He worked on the farm during the week and preached on Sunday. Within two years after Jacob's birth his father died. After three years his mother married again. Jacob's new dad was Mr. H. P. Andrus; the new home was established in a small village in north central Oregon.

The locality where anyone grows up, especially if it includes the entire period of one's childhood and youth, has a great deal to do with the development of the individual. Certainly this was true in the case of DeShazer. In view of this, our attention is arrested by the little, wind-swept prairie town of Madras, Oregon, with its population of less than three hundred, DeShazer's home from the time he was five years of age.

He did his entire elementary and high school work in Madras. Here he gained many ideas and learned something of the necessity for work, the privilege of citizenship, and the meaning of community responsibility. In school he studied the history of America and the world. In Sunday school and church he came into contact with the religious forces of the community.

Starting to high school in 1927 was a great experience. Mathematics seems to have been his favorite subject. Although somewhat shy, he became active in high school athletics. He played baseball and football. On Sundays he continued to go with his family to Sunday school in the local Free Methodist Church. If he stayed for the morning preaching service, he usually disappeared quickly after the benediction, rather than stay around and meet people. During the week, aside from time required for athletic practice, he spent most of his spare hours on the farm.

From several points of view the environment around Madras during those years was typical. Much like the parents of many other young people, DeShazer's parents were upright and religious. The local Sunday school and church tried to cooperate with the home in nurturing and fostering Christian concepts and the Christian way of life. As frequently found in many places, the public school, however, was rather neutral, if not indifferent, to any responsibility for cooperation with the home and the church in building Christian citizenship.

As a result, DeShazer was a typical American lad. He became self-reliant and somewhat independent. Increasingly he took more interest in the school than in the home. More and more he responded to the desires and activities of the young people outside the church circle, rather than to those within the church.

He did not openly rebel against his parents, but from time to time he would do things which he knew were not right. He smoked cigarettes and occasionally played hooky from school. For a time he almost developed a habit of stealing. Fortunately, this tendency was nipped in the bud. He was caught one time red-handed after he had stolen a man's suitcase. His mother and stepfather took the matter in hand, prayed with him and for him and then required that he make necessary apology and restitution. He reports, "It was hard to face my fine Christian parents and the neighbors after I had been reported as a thief. However, it was a very sure way to cure me of stealing."

High school graduation came in 1931. DeShazer was then between eighteen and nineteen years of age. He had no thought of entering college, so he began looking around for a permanent job.

But Madras offered little. Mention has been made above concerning certain typical factors in DeShazer's environment. This was not the case with respect to the community atmosphere in and around Madras. The entire locality was unique. The state of Oregon, historically, is well known as a western pioneer state. Originally, the name "Oregon" stood for the entire Northwest Territory.. Here was the end of the Oregon Trail. Unknown to many is the fact that there are today parts of Oregon which are as wild and as unimproved as a century ago. The state still boasts of numerous herds of wild horses.

Madras, the seat of Jefferson County, is located east of the Cascade Mountains on a high plateau. The climate is dry. The soil is volcanic in origin. The village, located a few miles east of the Deschutes River, about one hundred miles south of The Dalles, is the center of a grazing community. The surrounding country is rich in minerals and semi-precious stones. Petrified forests are numerous. Throughout the area are found many colorful agate and opal-filled nodules, usually called "thunder eggs," according to an Indian legend which maintains they were thrown out of Mt. Jefferson by the Spirits of Thunder. Many thousands of these specimens have been gathered, cut, and polished.

The entire area around Madras is rich with Indian lore and pioneer history. To the tourist who keeps to the main highway it is wonderful country. The scenery is superb. To the west, above the violet haze, looms Mt. Jefferson, more than 10,000 feet high, flanked on the north by Mt. Wilson and Mt. Hood and to the south by Three-Fingered Jack, Mt. Washington, the Three Sisters, and Broken Top. Along the highway to the south of Madras the traveler will see dwarfed juniper trees with distorted trunks and heavy evergreen foliage with silver-toned purple berries.

It is a vast country of space with almost continuous wind. Let the traveler get off the main highway, and it seems like leaving civilization behind and going back to the primitive. Here the ranch people reflect the hardihood which results from a struggle for existence in a semi-arid region, where neighbors are few and far between. As one travels over the unmarked roads across the prairies, he will occasionally find "stark ranch houses buried in the windy silence of the semi-treeless wastes, their owners devoted to a routine as solitary as it is monotonous." To these people, the automobile is man's greatest luxury. It makes possible an occasional return to civilization.

Anyone brought up in such surroundings and in such an atmosphere would be expected in his own make-up to reflect something of its spirit. So it is in the case of DeShazer. One of his acquaintances living in Madras who has known him since his childhood says, "He has a shy, but lovable personality, characterized by a sturdy determination which has insured his success at the tasks he has undertaken."

That phrase, "sturdy determination" describes something in DeShazer's life which can certainly be attributed to his environment. Such a trait is essential for survival in the country where he grew up.

Following graduation from high school, DeShazer tried to get work in the community around Madras. He wanted to save money for the establishment of a home of his own. For many months he worked for one ranch neighbor, then another. Wages at that time were a dollar per day and board. It seemed that the calls for money were beyond his resources. He found it impossible to save even a portion of his wages.

After some years he heard about an opening for a camp tender for sheep herders on the California-Nevada border. He accepted the position and worked there for two years. It was healthful and vigorous work. It required, of course, that he be outdoors most of the time. He fairly lived in the saddle, for it was his responsibility to carry supplies by pack-mule train into the mountains for the sheep herders. His comment regarding this experience is, "I enjoyed going to the mountains in the summer time and back to the deserts of Nevada in the winter time."

After two years, with little opportunity to spend money, he had accumulated one thousand dollars. With this "nest egg" in the bank, he felt that he was ready to go into business. Not wanting to go back to his home town, he located in Butte Falls, southwest of the Crater Lake area in Oregon. He decided to raise turkeys. Having made a considerable study of turkey raising, he felt he knew both the science and art involved. Subsequent developments made it clear, however, that he did not know some of the economic problems associated with such a speculative venture. He bought five hundred day-old turkeys. Throughout the weeks he cared for them day and night. He watched with great interest and anticipation their growth and development. Nothing was spared by way of providing correct food mixtures, proper shelter, and personal care.

By the holiday season his birds were in prime condition and ready for market. To his dismay, however, he found that the price of turkeys had taken a sudden drop from twenty-two cents a pound to only fourteen cents a pound. There was nothing he could do to avert financial disaster. Reluctantly he marketed his birds. When all bills were paid, not only was there no profit, but his entire one-thousand-dollar investment was gone. He had no money for a further business venture. This seems to have satisfied DeShazer's urge to go into business for himself. Once more he was confronted with the question, "Where to go and what to do?"

This period in the life of DeShazer illustrates how impossible it is for a person to be an isolationist. This does not refer to international isolationism, but rather to the impossibility of an individual being unaffected by forces having to do with his own government and his country.

During DeShazer's early life, though not in his memory, had been World War I with all of its tragedy. During the years prior to that first world conflict, American statesmen and international experts had been saying that an international conflict was impossible. But these men and all of their followers were soon to be disillusioned when the German Kaiser mobilized his troops. During the early days of that war, Americans felt that this country was safe because the Atlantic Ocean intervened. Then, too, we had the Monroe Doctrine! In spite of ominous war clouds, the leaders thought there would be no difficulty in keeping European enemies away from the Western Hemisphere.

But this sense of security was ill-founded. Soon practically the whole world was plunged into a deadly massacre, which wiped out nearly thirty million lives. An Armistice came in 1918—but it was only an Armistice. The seeds for another war had already been sown.

Little more than two decades had passed when the Armistice ended, and real war broke out again. We now call it World War II. No one knew, of course, in 1940, the extent to which this new outbreak would precipitate the whole world in another awful war. Statesmen, however, were very uneasy. America, once again, was trying to convince herself that she was safe, but at the same time the United States military leaders, hoping not to be caught unprepared as they were in 1917, called for and obtained "peace-time conscription."

DeShazer came to realize something of the situation. The United States Army was offering good pay. Then, too, he knew that being a single man he was a most eligible individual for army service in the event of war. Consequently, he enlisted. This was two years before Pearl Harbor. During this two-year period, DeShazer received basic training as an airplane mechanic and a bombardier. For a full year he was located at the McChord Field, just south of Tacoma, Washington.

CHAPTER II

IN THE ARMY—VOLUNTEERS FOR SECRET MISSION

The United States and Japan were allies during the First World War. Within a few years after the Armistice of 1918, however, evidences were mounting of a growing distrust and of tension between the two countries. The United States objected to Japan's aggressive policy in China. Furthermore, Japan was openly violating various international treaties. Behind the scenes, as subsequent records show, relations between the countries came almost to the breaking point several times. When the Second World War broke out in Europe and Japan sided with Germany, it further shook diplomatic relations. . . . then came Pearl Harbor!

Overnight hatreds against Japan in this country spread throughout the entire nation and rose to a white heat. Within a few weeks the Army on the West coast moved more than one hundred thousand persons of Japanese descent to concentration camps in the interior— this, in spite of the fact that half of these were American citizens.

Our national hatred toward the Japanese was further inflamed by information released by the State Department regarding the treachery and duplicity of the Japanese Ambassador in Washington, D. C., just before Pearl Harbor.

After Pearl Harbor came Wake, Guam, Manila, the Java Straits, and then Bataan. All of these names became fixed in the American mind, but always as defeats. The American people were wondering if there never would come news of something besides defeat. Our Navy and Air Force had been driven back. There was a pressing demand for the military authorities to do something quickly and emphatically to jar the Japanese leaders. One hardly dares to contemplate what we would have done to their cities if at that time we had had the A-bomb.

So it was, the military authorities decided to make an unprecedented raid on the Japanese mainland. Perhaps our bombers could set the flimsy houses in Tokyo aflame and start a great conflagration, such as followed the earthquake of 1923. In any event, the chance to make such an experiment with the possibility of jarring the Japanese and at the same time increasing the confidence of the American people in their own military leaders was worth the risk.

The matter was given careful thought. Extensive investigations were made regarding individual and social reactions of the Japanese people. Finally, it was agreed to make a military raid with care not to bomb the Imperial Palace. It was planned that nothing would be bombed except military installations. To carry out such a raid meant much planning and intense training.

Army life, prior to Pearl Harbor, included much routine, much moving about, but not much excitement. Two years of this kind of life produced the same effect on De-Shazer as on most other careless-minded youth. His comment on this period is no credit to him nor to the average American soldier.

> I had been living the kind of life that most of the enlisted men lived. I would associate with certain fellows and we would go to dances and drinking places to pass away our

> spare time. I feel ashamed of the events that took place in
> my life during those years. There is really no reason why
> anyone should want to live such a life. It does not lead
> to happiness.

After the bombing of Pearl Harbor, DeShazer was
sent to the air base at Columbia, South Carolina. Here
he was given further training as a bombardier. While
on duty one day in this capacity, word came for him to
report to his Captain. In the usual sense of the term
he had been a good soldier, but at the same time being
reprimanded was not an unknown experience to De-
Shazer. On this occasion he thought probably he was
scheduled for another reprimand and would be assigned
again to some form of K. P. duty.

To his surprise he found some fifteen or twenty other
fellows in the Captain's office when he arrived. Without
any preliminary statement the Captain asked them if they
would like to volunteer for a dangerous mission. The
whole thing was so sudden they hardly knew how to react.
They began to question regarding the nature of the mission, its destination and purpose. The Captain then explained something of its danger and hazard but said it was
so secret he could not tell them the details.

The more he talked, however, the more the proposition
sounded to the fellows like a great adventure. Everyone
who had reported to the Captain's office volunteered immediately. Others volunteered later.

As a result the whole program of DeShazer's daily
life was changed and that completely. The same was true
with the other volunteers. Excitement ran high. Soldiers
who had not volunteered looked on with a certain degree
of envy. Everything about the project was so mysterious
and secret that it daily gathered glamour and interest.

DeShazer was glad he had been chosen. He was not able to answer the query how it happened that he was "so fortunate"—but God had a purpose!

Within a few days the volunteers for this dangerous mission were sent to Eglin Field in Florida. Here they were subjected to intensive training in all types of air maneuvers. DeShazer continued his training as airplane mechanic and bombardier. It was obvious that the secret mission would require low flying and bombing, for much time was given during this intensive training period to flying airplanes very low. DeShazer's pilot, Lieutenant William Farrow, and the other members of the crew almost made a sport of their practice. Sometimes they would fly so low across fields that they would have to rise to go over fences. At other times they would fly along and inside a ditch so low that the banks of the ditch were higher than the airplane itself. Experiences were many, hazards were numerous, and accidents were frequent.

General James Doolittle, at that time a Lieutenant-Colonel, had been placed in charge of the expedition. He went to Washington to receive special orders and special instructions. Here he was told he could have practically anything he felt necessary in order to carry out the mission successfully. His requests were to have top priority. The cost was not to be a matter of consideration. The raid itself was to be the all-important thing.

With the return of Doolittle from Washington, the training was greatly intensified. Airplanes were loaded with heavy dud bombs, and the pilots would try to get the planes off the ground by flying very short distances.

This program of training continued for a full month. Then came the order to leave Florida and go to San

Francisco. The crews turned the trip across the United
States into a practice flight. Most of the way they flew
very low. DeShazer's comment regarding this cross-
country flight suggests an initial excitement far different
from that of the final raid.

> When we got to Texas and New Mexico, we could see
> the cattle in the fields. Our pilots would fly low in order
> to frighten the animals. It was great sport to see them
> put their tails in the air and run for all they were worth.
> We thought that was lots of fun and were glad to be in the
> Army and see something exciting.

On April 1—April Fool's Day—1942, the airplanes,
sixteen in number, were hoisted to the flight deck of the
aircraft carrier, *U. S. S. Hornet.* They were B-25 North
American bombers. DeShazer's plane was the last one,
No. 16. It was anchored to the flight deck with a portion
of the tail assembly hanging over the stern.

The next day, April 2, the *Hornet* left San Francisco
Bay and sailed out under the Golden Gate Bridge. It was
high noon, and a spirit of adventure and celebration possessed everyone on board.

From time to time other ships joined the convoy
until the entire Task Force consisted of twelve ships: the
aircraft carrier *Hornet*, another aircraft carrier, the *En-
terprise,* two cruisers, two tankers, and six destroyers.

They were only about ten miles off shore when the announcement blared forth over the public address system
on the *Hornet* describing something of the expedition.
They were told that the objective was the bombing of
Japan. They were also told that they were not going to
stop at any other port before the bombers would be
launched for the raid.

Sailors and airmen alike began to cheer. Great was

the commotion. This is understandable when one remembers there were over two thousand sailors on the *Hornet*. In addition to these were the one-hundred-sixty Air Corps men assigned to General Doolittle's squadron. The entire group was celebrating, not only because they were participating in a great adventure but also because they were sharing in the feeling of many that the bombing of Japan would help bring to a halt the awful aggression of the Japanese.

American schools are noted for their emphasis upon peace and international good will. Notwithstanding this, these men, although indoctrinated in the American schools to hate war, were ready to fight. Speaking of this experience later, DeShazer says,

> I sensed a fighting spirit among these men. We did not have to have speeches to point out what was wrong with Japan. Every person seemed to know that Japan was an outlaw and would have to be forced to surrender. The Japanese were taking things that didn't belong to them. They had started the war. These American men were ready to fight against such unrighteousness.

The men felt that they were going on a real crusade. Theirs was the opportunity and the task to change the bad news of war to good news. They felt that given this opportunity they would be able to make a vital blow against the Japanese war machine. It seems that every fellow was thrilled with the thought of being a part of the expedition. The sailors on the *Hornet* looked on the Air Corps men with envy. It is interesting to note in this connection that the eighty airmen held in reserve in the event anyone in the first line of volunteers "lost heart" were all disappointed. No one became ill, and no one "backed out." Thus, no replacements were made.

The pilot of DeShazer's plane, Lieutenant William Farrow, was six feet six inches tall. He was from the South. The co-pilot, Lieutenant Hite, was from Texas; the navigator, Lieutenant Barr, from New York, and the rear gunner, Sergeant Spaatz, from Kansas. The bombardier was Sergeant Jacob DeShazer, at that time a corporal. Naturally, these men became well acquainted during their period of intensive training. In those days, however, they did not realize fully how well they would become acquainted during the next three years. Speaking of their ability, DeShazer said modestly, "We found out that we were the least trained of any of the crews of the B-25s."

DeShazer had had many experiences as an Army man. He also had had many experiences in the Army Air Corps. He had frequently wondered, however, what life would be like on a ship. This was his first contact with the Navy. Even this experience on the sea amounted to little more than two weeks—but what a two weeks! Here he was, on an aircraft carrier and a member of a favored few!

On his very first night on shipboard DeShazer was called out for guard duty. About midnight when every thing was dark he apparently lost some of his courage. Even though he had a 45 pistol strapped to his side, he began to have strange feelings as he contemplated the future. He says,

> I began to wonder how many more days I was to spend in this world. Maybe I wasn't so fortunate after all to get to go on this trip. I tried to comfort myself with statistics which I could recall. I reminded myself that only 50,000 Americans had been killed in the First World War. I shuddered to think where I would go if I was to die.

During the day, however, things were different. Something of interest was happening every hour. A part of the time the airmen would watch the Marines as they practised with anti-aircraft guns on the ship. Sometimes the gunners would climb into their own airplanes and shoot the guns. At times they would rig up a kite for a target as they would practise shooting. Men of the Air Corps were given the privilege of going about the *Hornet* looking at the engines, the various quarters and the like.

One day, while DeShazer was in the engine room looking at a small opening, a sailor asked him what he thought he was looking at. DeShazer replied, "Out of the side of the ship." The sailor answered, "You're looking right straight up the smoke stack of the *Hornet*." There was not a trace of smoke, and DeShazer was surprised to learn how the view up the smoke stack could be observed with the use of mirrors. The airmen and sailors fraternized much during these days, and according to DeShazer, "They found that the sailors weren't such bad fellows after all."

Seals swimming alongside the ship were of great interest. The albatross, particularly, drew DeShazer's attention. In recalling these experiences he says,

The albatross followed us, flying on tireless wings. I watched their graceful flying each day. It seemed strange that they could keep up to the aircraft carrier and never appear to move their wings. I studied aero-dynamics in the army schools, but I did not understand the flying ease of the albatross. I did notice that their tail feathers acted similar to a rudder on an airplane. These strange birds didn't have to go to school to learn how to fly. They were shown the way to fly by their Creator.

In looking back over those days, DeShazer made other observations. Evidently, being out on the great Pacific Ocean where nothing was seen for days except the blue water, which itself seemed to be continually moving, he became meditative. He says,

> I felt a longing for something which is hard to describe. I did not know what that longing was at that time. The Creator was certainly trying to manifest Himself to me by this great display of His creation. Job 12:9 tells us, "Who knoweth not in all these that the hand of the Lord hath wrought this?" I longed for fellowship with this Creator. I did not know at that time how God would gladly fellowship with his creation. I did not realize that God would gladly fellowship with me, if I would meet the conditions written in the Bible.

One very interesting sight to all the men on board the *Hornet* was the re-fueling of the ships from the tankers. To re-fuel at sea is a difficult and dangerous undertaking. One day an oil tanker pulled alongside the *Hornet* for this purpose. The sea was unusually rough. Waves of water were actually breaking over the tanker itself. Suddenly the nose of the tanker dipped down into a huge, rolling wave. When it came up riding the waves again, it was discovered that a man was overboard. He was prepared, however, for such an eventuality, for he was wearing a life vest. Quickly, someone from on deck threw an inflated raft to him. The sailor seized this. Soon he was seen sitting on the raft and waving his hand as the *Hornet* kept on going. Word was quickly sent to one of the other ships in the convoy, and the unhappy sailor was picked up by one of the destroyers. An announcement was later made over the public address system that the sailor was uninjured.

Sunday, April 5, was Easter Sunday. In keeping

with the day an Easter service was held aboard each ship. Reports say it was surprising how many men showed up. DeShazer, however, was not interested. He did not attend.

The convoy kept going day after day. Included in the routine were talks by various Naval officers who told about Japan, the Japanese Army and Navy, Japanese economic conditions and the general layout. Much attention was also given to Japan's industrial set-up, her water systems, fire hazards, balloon barrages and the like. Much time, too, was spent in idleness, card playing, and shooting craps.

CHAPTER III

GENERAL QUARTERS ALARM ON BOARD THE *U.S.S. HORNET*

Prior to Friday, April 17, the men on the ships other than the *Hornet* did not know the nature of the mission. On that day, however, the Commander of the Task Force made the following announcement: "This Task Force has been directed to proceed to a position 400 miles east of Japan. The Army bombers will be launched from the *U.S.S. Hornet*. They will bomb Tokyo." Now, for the first time, the sailors and the men on the other eleven ships in the convoy knew the purpose of the secret trip.

When the announcement came over the loud speakers, most of the men were seated at lunch. At first everyone seemed to be frozen to his seat. Then spirits brightened, and on some ships gay little songs were cheerfully sung. Some of these to the tune of *Snow White* went, "Hi, ho, we're off to Tokyo. We will bomb and blast and come back fast." Perhaps the cheeriness was essentially "whistling in the dark" for everywhere there was unmistakable tenseness. A strange feeling seemed to fill the air. It was evidenced on every ship, whether on the bridge, in the lookouts, in the crew's mess, or in the quarters. A question arose in the mind of each one, "How close to Tokyo can we get without being spotted?" This question, of course, had to go unanswered, at least for the time.

Throughout the hours of the evening and night everything was grim and silent and yet the ships, under forced

On "Hornet" Awaiting Orders to Take Off
General Doolittle with Captain Mitscher and airmen ready for call to "Man Your Planes."

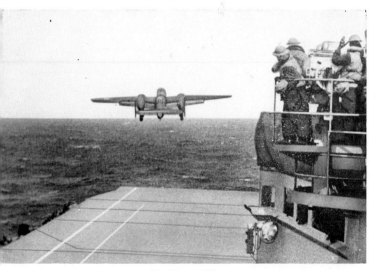

The "Take-off"
One of the 16 B-25 Bombers as it took off the "Hornet" for the first
U. S. air raid on Japan.

General Doolittle
Autographed picture given DeShazer
by the General.

Tokyo Burns
U. S. Bombers set many fires in Tokyo.

Bomb-scarred Tokyo
As it appeared toward end of war. The devastation was almost complete.
Only steel structure buildings were left standing.

draft, were steaming ever westward. Everyone felt the zero hour was not far away. The sea was heavy, the sky was overcast, white-capped rollers flew over the tossing bows of the battleships. Spray splashed over the flight decks of the carriers. The lookouts were being soaked in the driving rain. The men in the ward room of the *Hornet* spent most of their time looking at a big map on the wall. Few words were spoken and fewer jokes. Finally, the men turned in, but most of them turned in with their clothes on.

No one knew exactly when the order would be given for Doolittle to take off. We now know that the original plan was for them to take off late on the evening of Saturday, April 18, so as to arrive in Japan early Sunday morning and go on across to China so as to land before dark on that day. But these plans were changed. This changed the entire outcome of the raid, particularly with respect to DeShazer and his crew mates.

The first factor which had a part in changing the plans was the sighting of two Japanese surface craft. It was believed certain they were a part of the patrol maintained by the Japanese. Immediately a General Quarters Alarm was given. This was about 3 :15, the morning of Saturday, April 18. A General Quarters Alarm is a piercing Clang! Clang! Clang! which is a call for all hands to go to battle stations. Immediately there was a rushing within the ships. Men poured up through the hatches, and in the blackness covers came off guns. Ammunition was made ready.

The alarm, of course, aroused the Army Air Corps men on the *Hornet*. DeShazer and the other Doolittle men were quickly up and waiting. In the meantime they were watching the proceedings. Fortunately, the enemy ships apparently did not see the convoy. The Task Force at that time was nearly nine-hundred miles east of Japan. It was hoped to keep on sailing until about four-hundred miles from Japan before launching the airplanes. There was constant fear, however, that some patrol boat of the Japanese might sight them.

Shortly after dawn, a Japanese fishing vessel was sighted, and low on the horizon, two Japanese ships which appeared to be destroyers. The Commander of the Task Force now felt it was impossible to keep his presence un-known. He was reasonably certain that these ships had seen the convoy and of course had radioed its strength and position to Tokyo.

Suddenly one of Halsey's cruisers started shooting. This was real warfare. The big guns were booming, and it looked as though the whole side of the cruiser was on fire. Although the seas were heavy, making accurate firing difficult, the fishing boat quickly sank, one end sticking straight up toward the sky as it went down. Another cruiser left the convoy and took after the Japa-nese ships over the horizon where it disappeared from sight. After a time when the cruiser reappeared, it was announced throughout the convoy that both enemy ships had been sunk, and that although the cruiser had attempted to pick up survivors, all the men had gone down before it arrived at the scene of the wreckage.

A decision had to be made. Should the convoy attempt to go in closer to Japan or should the bombers take off? At about eight o'clock in the morning the crisp and sig-nificant order was given. The words which came over the *Hornet's* loud speakers stated: "Army Personnel, man your planes." This was repeated several times. On the loud speakers on the accompanying ships announcement was being broadcast, "*Hornet* preparing to launch bombers for attack on Tokyo."

Those on the convoy, including officers, cooks, engineers, and seemingly everyone else on board crowded the decks of the other ships watching what was happening on the *Hornet*.

On the flight deck of the *Hornet,* however, there was methodical movement. Each man, of course, was wondering whether he would now have any chance at all, but there was no time to stop to figure that out. Some pleasantries were exchanged. DeShazer's pilot came by and asked him if he knew how to row a boat. All realized with approximately eight hundred miles away from any land at all—and that enemy land—a boat or some other device would be necessary if they expected to live out their natural lives. Another sergeant, just as he was crawling into the rear compartment of his plane, shouted to DeShazer, "We just got one chance in a thousand of making it." Again, no time to think about it! There was work to do.

Sergeant Spaatz was filling up the gas tanks and making last minute check-ups. DeShazer was helping to load the bombs. Everyone was anxious to see how the airplanes would get into the air. All eyes were on General Doolittle, who was the first to take off. With fifteen planes behind him, he had a very short distance for his take-off. As a matter of fact, he had only about 450 feet. The shortest run at any of the practice fields for a take-off had been approximately seven hundred feet. It looked impossible. The ship pitched and the runway tossed up and down. Men on the accompanying vessels, through the rain and motor exhaust could dimly see Doolittle's plane poised at the take-off position.

Doolittle knew what he was doing. His motors raced
faster. The aircraft carrier was cutting into the waves at
a speed that had seldom been equaled in Naval history.
The wind would almost blow a person off the deck.
The airplane needed very little added speed before the
air speed was enough to lift it. As the forward part of
the aircraft carrier went up, the Navy man gave the signal. The brakes were released. The airplane fairly
jumped into the air. When the *Hornet's* bow came down,
the airplane was seen in the air. It soon rose to an altitude, leveled off and Doolittle circled over the *Hornet* in
a farewell salute. Cheers rose from the throats of those
who watched.

A B-25 could take off the deck of the *Hornet*, but
there was no possible way for it to land back on the
carrier. Once in the air it was necessary to stay aloft
or crash into the sea.

A few minutes after General Doolittle's plane another
plane took off, then another and another. One plane
looked as if it would not make it. It disappeared over
the end of the deck, and gasps were heard from the spec-
tators, but it came up with roaring engines, its nose
sticking straight up toward the sky. Soon the sky was
filled with planes—all sixteen.

To those remaining on the *Hornet* and on the decks of
the other ships of the convoy, it was a wonderful sight.
Sixteen medium American bombers with their beautiful lines, the American insignia painted boldly on the
wings and fusilages, the roar of their twin motors, gave a
real sense of pride.

But Sergeant DeShazer had some real experiences in
his take-off. He with his comrades was in airplane No.
16. Because of the crowded conditions his plane was

pushed to the stern of the deck, the tail actually hanging over. Just before they were ready to taxi into the take-off position, suddenly, perhaps because of the wind, the nose of the airplane was rising up off the deck. The tail end was going down. It looked as though the plane were about to drop off into the sea. Sailors quickly tied some lines to the nose of the airplane, but these broke. It was a most critical moment. Nothing but courage and man-power would save the plane.

Every man who could get a hand-hold crowded in and hung on to the front end of the airplane. DeShazer himself was trying to assist. By sheer grit, stamina, and human strength the plane was held on the deck. A tragedy, however, occurred during this excitement. Unfortunately, one of the sailors backed into the propeller of the airplane. Lieutenant Farrow already had his motors going at fairly high speed. One of the sailor's arms was completely cut off. DeShazer assisted others in carrying him to one side so that the plane could taxi into position for the take-off.

Before this excitement bombs had been loaded, but, since the tail end was sticking out so far, it had been impossible to load the crew's bags and other equipment. After getting into the take-off position, it was necessary to finish loading the plane. This was most difficult because of the tremendous gale that was blowing across the deck. Imagine DeShazer's surprise, however, when finally getting into position in the nose of the airplane, to find that something had broken the plastic nose of the plane. Instead of being wind tight and rounded, it contained a jagged hole more than a foot in diameter just at the right of the gun mount. No one had noticed it before. When it had happened, no one knew. Undoubtedly, it had occurred when the plane had bounced around and bumped into the plane ahead of it when this forward plane was getting into position to take off.

In any event, there was little which DeShazer could do, for at that very moment the pilot was speeding his engines for the take-off. The plane was shaking with the terrific speed of the motors. The Navy man was all set to give the signal for the take-off. Admiral Halsey still had the *Hornet* headed straight into the wind. Further delay was impossible. An order had been received to push the plane overboard if it could not take off. DeShazer buckled on the safety belt and tried to sit easy as the plane went down the runway. It was a perfect take-off. This last plane like the first circled over the *Hornet* for a farewell salute.

As this last plane started westward, DeShazer observed that the *Hornet* already had changed its course. With the other vessels of the convoy it had started back home. Its job was done. The "raiders" were off.

DeShazer told the pilot over the intercommunication phone that there was a big hole in the nose of the plane. Lieutenant Farrow sent his co-pilot, Lieutenant Hite, forward to investigate. They tried putting a coat in the hole, but the wind took it away. They finally had to give up. There was now nothing to do but to try to reach Japan, drop their bombs and then—perhaps disappear forever. It was a dark hour. They knew their gas supply would be short at the very best, but now with a hole in the nose of the plane, the streamline effect of the B-25 was greatly reduced.

DeShazer's plane was one of three planes under the immediate command of Colonel John Hilger who was in plane No. 14. These three planes were supposed to fly in formation until they reached Japan. Lieutenant Smith with plane No. 15 was on Colonel Hilger's right wing and Lieutenant Farrow, with Plane No. 16 was on his left. Colonel Hilger, however, reports that he lost sight of Farrow soon after the take-off when they passed through a rain storm. Evidently the slow speed of Farrow's plane because of the broken plane nose was the reason for his failure to keep in formation.

CHAPTER IV

BOMBS JAPAN—BAILS OUT—CAPTURED

Lieutenant Farrow with his crew of four including De-Shazer left the *Hornet* at about 9:20 A.M. In spite of their slow speed they reached Japan about 1:00 o'clock that afternoon. The trip was uneventful. Very few airplanes were seen, and these apparently did not notice the American bomber approaching. Much of the distance over open water was flown at a very low altitude, perhaps only 100 feet.

When Japan was reached, however, they found high clouds. In order to get over the mountains, it was necessary to fly up through the clouds at an altitude of about 7,000 feet. To their surprise they found people living on these mountains. Much of the flying at this altitude was just above the tree tops. The Japanese people, of course, were surprised. Apparently, they did not understand that this was an enemy airplane, for some of them waved a greeting. At one time, DeShazer noticed an old gray-bearded gentleman walking along a mountain pathway using a cane. He glanced back at the plane and threw himself flat on the ground as the plane rushed by only a few feet above him.

The target which was assigned to DeShazer's plane was not Tokyo but Nagoya about three hundred miles south of the capital city. When they reached Nagoya the day was beautiful and the sun was shining. DeShazer reports that it did not look much like the maps they had been shown. As they approached the first target in Nagoya, the pilot said, "Get set to drop the bombs at five hundred feet. There is the first target." DeShazer, in charge of the actual bombing, looked straight ahead and saw some oil storage tanks. The plane went right over the top of the highest tank at five hundred feet. DeShazer looked down the "angle line" that, for precaution, had been substituted for a bomb sight, and let the incendiary bomb go. He tried to drop another bomb on another tank and then suddenly noticed that three bombs had been released instead of two. Let us listen to DeShazer's own story:

We were making a complete turn, and I smelled smoke. I wanted to see how an oil refinery looked when it was on fire. To the left of us I saw where the first bombs had dropped. There was fire all over the tank, but it had not blown up yet. What I was smelling, however, was powder of the shells that were being shot at us instead of the bombs I had dropped. I had noticed a little black smoke cloud right in front of us, and evidently the hole in the nose of our airplane allowed the smoke to come inside.

We went over a big factory-looking building and dropped the last incendiary. We skimmed along down a valley on our way out to the ocean. I was getting ready to shoot. There is something about being shot at that makes you want to shoot back. I had read in the newspapers one time about a German aviator shooting at French people, and I thought it was a mean thing to do. I made up my mind while on the *Hornet* that I would not shoot at civilians. But after they shot at us, I changed my mind.

I saw a man standing in a fishing boat, waving as we came along. He thought that we were Japanese. I thought that I would show him that we weren't. I shot a few shots near him, and the poor fellow stopped waving. I wasn't a very good shot, however, and therefore no harm was done.

We flew along the coast of Japan intending to fly on the 13th parallel to Choo Chow Lishui, in China. We saw several of the other B-25s, but did not follow any of them. When night came, we saw dimly the coast line of China, but the fog was so thick we could not tell what part of China we were approaching.

Our navigator, Lieutenant Barr, was doing lots of paper work. He said we should be over Choo Chow Lishui. The pilot circled, calling on the radio all the time. No answer came back. The fog cleared off a little. We could see a town below but no airfield.

In the tanks we had gasoline enough for only one hour. We had to do something and Lieutenant Farrow was anxious to save the B-25. It was a good old gas burner. With a hole in the nose it had already stayed in the air for more than thirteen hours. By flying beyond Japanese-held territory we could get to Keyon in Free China, where more gasoline was stored. We might be able to see the airfield or get a response from the Chinese radio operator. After we had flown for one hour, we saw a town. Our gasoline was nearly gone. We circled the town, calling and looking for lights from an airfield but to no avail. Finally Lieutenant Farrow said, "We gotta jump." It was 11:40 p.m. by the same time as when we left the *Hornet*. The airplane was at an altitude of 3,000 feet. I watched Lieutenant Barr go first, and then I jumped.

It wasn't exactly a jump. I put my legs out and the wind knocked them against the fusilage of the airplane so hard that I had to push against the door frame in order to get out of the opening on the lower side of the fusilage. I gave a shove and then watched the plane go over my head. I lost my hat as the wind was shrieking over me. When the plane had gone beyond me, I pulled the rip cord and was given a hard but welcome jerk as the parachute immediately opened. I watched the light go out of sight from the opening in the fusilage of the plane. Soon the sound of the motors died out. Everywhere I looked it was dark. The fog was thick around me, and I felt a strange sensation of loneliness.

I had no way of knowing that I was coming down since I could not see the ground and there was no sensation of wind since the parachute had opened. I began to wonder if I would have to sit up there all night. Suddenly I hit the earth with an awful jolt. The place where I landed was the final resting grounds of a Chinaman. I threw my arms around that mound of dirt and gave it a big hug. I was glad to be back on the ground even if it was a good long way from the U. S. A. I saw several mounds of dirt and noticed that I was on a knoll. Then I realized it was a Chinese graveyard. All around were rice fields which were under water at that time of the year. I found out later that at the very time I was coming down in the parachute my mother was awakened from her sleep and was praying for me.

DeShazer was too stunned to realize that some ribs were fractured in the landing. He was able, however, to move about and to walk. He shot his pistol into the air several times, but there was no response from any direction. He then cut the parachute to pieces with his knife and used a portion of the silk to protect his head from the rain. He started walking. It was difficult to find his way around the rice fields, for everywhere it was muddy and slippery.

He does not know how long he walked, but in due time he came to a little brick building which apparently had been used as a shrine by some Chinese farmer. It was beside running water and had irons to be used for burning incense. Although it was very small, he was able to clear out enough space to get in and barely have room to sit. It was a shelter from the rain. Through sheer weariness he fell asleep and did not waken until daylight. Immediately he began to look for a road.

After walking some distance, he came to a path. As he walked along this path, he began meeting people. No one, however, seemed to be interested, and no one seemed to be excited or suspicious. This made him think that he might be in Chinese territory. From time to time he would stop a man and try to get him to tell whether it was Japanese territory or not. Seemingly no one understood his questions, or perhaps they were unwilling to say. He finally came to a store. He went in. Here he wrote a few words on a pad, but the Chinese storekeeper could give him no information.

Once again he took to the road and walked for several hours. Finally, he came to a main road and a telephone line. This was a source of real encouragement for it appeared he might be able to get help. The few hours of walking along Chinese farms and seeing Chinese homes, gave DeShazer his first sight of the awful living conditions of the Chinese.

> I could see inside their mud houses. Chickens, pigs, and children wading around together in filthy mud inside the house. The people had heads about the size of a four-year old child in America. The skin on their faces was wrinkled and old looking. I didn't expect to find out much from them. I didn't care to ask them for anything to eat although I was getting very hungry.

He continued walking down the main highway. In due time he came to a group of houses which obviously constituted a military base. He saw some soldiers outside washing clothes in a ditch. That was one time he wished he knew how to tell the Chinese from the Japanese. Were these soldiers friends or were they enemies? Should he go up to them and make himself known? No, he thought best not to do so.

He walked farther down the road until he came to another house. Gathering all the courage possible, he went to this house to make inquiry. Inside he found two young soldiers playing with some Chinese children. He started talking by sign language and, of course, also used English. He would use the word, "America," and point to himself. He then pointed to one of the soldiers and asked, "China or Japan?" The soldier replied, "China." He had his misgivings. Fear seemed to take possession of him. He fixed his 45 pistol so a bullet was in the chamber and the hammer drawn back. He knew the pistol contained seven good bullets, and he was ready to shoot it out if they were Japanese.

As he stood there, he began to feel perhaps it was better for him to leave the house and go on his way. Just as he started to back away toward the door, to his consternation he found ten soldiers, armed with bayonets, pistols and swords, standing at the entrance. He yelled at them, "China or Japan?" As he yelled, he was holding his hand on the pistol. Instantly, they hollered back, "China." DeShazer says, "I didn't want to start shooting at the Chinese, so I let them come in."

The soldiers came in, succeeded in getting him to shake hands, patted him on the back and tried to act like old-time friends. Even though it was difficult to talk to each other, they succeeded in getting him to go with them down the road to a camp. As they were walking along, they stopped for a moment, and to DeShazer's further consternation he found that a bayonet was against his back. Suddenly, guns were pointing at him from every direction. The leader of the group then reached over and took his pistol from the holster.

In due time they reached the camp. The officer who met them seemed somewhat friendly. He talked abusively to the other soldiers who came out to look at him, and they quickly disappeared into their houses like a bunch of frightened children. DeShazer was seated at a table, and a fellow began asking him questions. The questioner knew English fairly well. It was now perfectly obvious to DeShazer that the men were Japanese, not Chinese. When this fact dawned upon him, he was completely discouraged. His own description of this experience indicates that his feelings were at an even lower ebb than months later when he was being severely punished in prison. Nevertheless he tried to let on that he did not realize that they were Japanese.

In this state of mind, he seems to have been both morose and courageous. To practically every question which was asked, his answer was, "I don't know" or "I won't tell." In his own words he says:

> The Japanese finally found out that I wouldn't tell them anything they wanted to know. So they asked me if I wanted to eat. I told them that that wasn't a bad idea. They gave me some hot cakes with apple butter. Perhaps it was not apple butter, but that is as close to it as I can describe it. The taste was different from anything that I had ever eaten. It had an Oriental tang. The tea and food, however, made me feel a lot better.

He saw pictures of some high-ranking officers on the wall and asked the interpreter the names of the officers, thinking this would give him some idea for sure where he was. The interpreter mentioned several names, but they meant nothing to DeShazer. Finally, it seems that the officer in charge, thinking that DeShazer knew for certain that they were Japanese, instructed the interpreter to tell him point blank, "You are in the hands of the Japanese." Now all hope was gone, but questionings continued.

"Aren't you afraid?" asked the interpreter.

"What should I be afraid of?" he asked.

For some reason or other this question brought up the question of American slang. They had an interesting discussion regarding this subject.

A short time later he was taken to another town. He reports that in spite of all his efforts he was never able to find out the name of either of these towns. Here, however, he learned that four of his comrades had also been picked up. They met for the first time the next morning and were photographed together on the front steps of a building.

CHAPTER V

INQUISITION IN TOKYO

DeShazer almost lost track of time. How many hours after he had bailed out of his plane before being placed on another plane as a prisoner, he does not know. At any rate, he and his comrades were placed together in a plane similar to a D-3 transport plane and flown to another city. Evidently the distance was great, for they were in the air a good share of a day. We now know this trip took them to Nanking, China.

In the evening they were taken off the plane and had their first experience of being in an Oriental prison. The cells were made of wooden bars, placed straight up and down. The room was bare except for a wooden box for a toilet. Guards walked back and forth in front of the cell. Here someone took DeShazer's wrist watch, which he never saw again. A little later he was led into a room where a group of Japanese officers began questioning him again. Describing this experience, DeShazer says:

> One of the officers, using lots of slang, said that I had better talk. He said that these were mean people, and they would torture me until I did talk. I was still blindfolded as I had been most of the time for over twelve hours and hadn't eaten all day. I had been asked questions at every opportunity, but I would always tell them that I wouldn't talk. Sometimes they would tell me about places in America where Japan had bombed and taken possession of property; then they would come up very close to my face and open their mouths and laugh.
>
> I was then led into a room, and the blindfold was re-

General Tojo
He persuaded Emperor to commute
DeShazer's sentence.

General Sugiyama
He demanded DeShazer and comrades
be executed.

A Japanese Prison
Similar to, though not identical with, the prison where DeShazer was kept
in solitary confinement.

The Great Buddha
This idol was erected in 1252 at Kamakura.

An Actual Execution
DeShazer was spared by reprieve from the Emperor.

Prisoners Are Released
Japanese guards bow as American prisoners of war are being released at close of war.

moved. A little Japanese of stocky build was standing behind a table smoking a cigar, rubbing his hands together and talking really fast in Japanese. Several others were in the room. The man behind the table said through the interpreter, "I am the kindest judge in all China. I want to treat you real good. Everywhere I have the reputation of being the kindest judge in all China." We sat down and the kind judge looked at a paper.

Then, through the interpreter, the following conversation took place.

Judge: How do you pronounce H-O-R-N-E-T?

DeShazer: Hornet.

Judge: And that is the aircraft carrier you flew off to bomb Japan, isn't it?

DeShazer: I won't talk.

Judge: Colonel Doolittle was your Commanding Officer, wasn't he?

DeShazer: I won't talk.

The judge hit the table with his fist and yelled in Japanese. The interpreter translated the judge's words, "When you speak, look me straight in the eye!"

DeShazer says that after that when questions were asked, he looked the judge straight in the eye when giving his answer. Evidently, he was able to look him out of countenance, for he reports the judge lowered his eyes and looked away. Finally, DeShazer was told that in Japan it was considered a great honor for the judge to get to cut the prisoner's head off.

At this point the judge, looking at DeShazer, said (speaking in English this time), "Tomorrow morning at sunrise I'm going to have the honor of cutting your head off." As the reader considers such an experience, knowing the sequel, it seems somewhat humorous. Certainly, it was far from humorous to DeShazer. In view of the tenseness of the situation and impending tragedy, one is amazed at DeShazer's answer. From his own account we read:

> I told him I thought it would be a great honor to me if the kindest judge in China cut my head off. The judge and others laughed for the first time, and a little later I was taken to my cell.
>
> I lay in the cell all night, blindfolded, handcuffed, without blankets. The next morning at sunrise I was led out of my cell. I had no breakfast. The blindfold was taken off, and the handcuffs were removed. I looked around for the judge with his weapon of execution, but I saw a fellow with a camera, and everyone was smiling. After the picture was taken, I was loaded onto a Japanese two-motored transport. Again I was blindfolded, handcuffed, and tied with ropes. I could hear some of my companions talking, but I was not able to say anything to them. Soon after the plane took to the air, we were given some good ham sandwiches.

DeShazer was due to experience more—much more— of the misery of war. It was a new experience to be a captive and no longer to have freedom—to be moved and pushed about according to the whims of the enemy.

The flight carried them for several hours over water. In due time, they were again over land, and DeShazer heard the Japanese talking excitedly and, as is sometimes their custom, drawing air through their teeth. Surreptitiously, DeShazer peeked out through his blindfold and saw Mt. Fuji. By this he knew he was over Japan. A little later they landed and were taken by automobile to another prison.

Again DeShazer and his comrades were subjected to questions. It was obvious the Japanese had found some papers that told the number of airplanes and the names of the crews on each airplane. The name, *Hornet,* also, was apparently on some of the papers. Evidently someone had not destroyed all the information as everyone had been instructed by Colonel Doolittle. DeShazer and his comrades were questioned in great detail regarding the aircraft carrier and the information which had been found on these papers.

One of DeShazer's comrades, Lieutenant George Barr, was a real curiosity to the Japanese because he was six feet two inches tall and had red hair. Japanese soldiers and Japanese people would come and look at him again and again in his cell as though he were on exhibition. At times they would ask him what he ate and drank in order to get that color of hair. He was the first red-headed person they had ever seen. When Lieutenant Barr was asked how he came to be there he would say that he had jumped out of an airplane and, when he hit the ground, he landed on his head. He said that he couldn't remember anything since that had happened.

The unexpected and bold attempt of the American airmen to bomb Japan was a great shock to General Headquarters at Tokyo. General Sugiyama, Chief of the General Staff, was greatly enraged at what he called "indiscriminate" bombing and declared:

> "The air raids are a matter of strategic military operation. They should come under the jurisdiction of the military staff headquarters. All the investigations and punishments in regard to the raids will be conducted by our military staff headquarters in Tokyo."

Of the sixteen raiding planes, two unfortunately entered the areas which were occupied by Japanese forces. The captured flyers of these two planes were eight in number. Five of them, including DeShazer, were first sent to Nanking, and three were sent to Shanghai. The

Japanese military authorities in China promptly notified
the Tokyo military headquarters regarding the capture.
General Headquarters promptly issued an order to have
the captured flyers sent to Tokyo for questioning. This
was done.

Obviously, the Doolittle air raid had taken the Japanese military authorities off guard. It was a new experience for them; consequently there was no precedent.
The question immediately arose whether the captured
airmen should be treated as war "prisoners" or as war
"criminals."

From the very outset, General Sugiyama felt they
were war criminals and should be executed without delay.

As a result of his order, General Shigera Sawada,
the Commanding Officer of the 13th Japanese Army sta-
tioned at Shanghai, sent the eight men to Tokyo for trial.

Very soon it developed that there was a definite difference of opinion between the military headquarters and
the Japanese War Department. General Sugiyama was
insisting upon the death penalty for all eight captives.
General Tojo, who was then Premier, felt this was too
severe. Besides, Japan at the time had no law which declared the death penalty to air raiders who might be
captured. In spite of Premier Tojo's apparent leniency,
he quickly ordered the authorities in Japan to establish a
law which would impose the death penalty in order to
apply it if need be to the captured Doolittle flyers. This
is one way General Tojo planned to threaten other Allied
flyers, should they be captured. Such treatment was entirely different from that given to ordinary captives
whose punishment—after a mock trial—was usually torture and imprisonment.

The conflict between the military leaders with respect to procedure to be followed delayed the expected trial day after day and week after week. In the meantime, however, the prisoners were called before an examining board again and again. All told there were eighteen days of such inquisition. During these days the entire eight men were unable to carry on conversations. The five men from DeShazer's plane knew that three men had been captured from another plane but did not know the circumstances of their landing or their capture. In the intervals between the questionings, they could hear their voices in another part of the prison.

In the Tokyo War Tribunal Court held after the close of the war, a Mr. Rykichi Tanaka, in testifying concerning the controversy said:

> At the time when Mr. Sato, the Chief of the Bureau of Military Affairs, reported that the Army Headquarters decided to sentence the flyers to death, General Tojo, the War Minister, promptly opposed this decision, stating that the action might result in extremely unfavorable consequences to the Japanese Nationals interned in America. For this reason the verdict was postponed for a considerable length of time.

Further questions and answers which were given at the Tokyo War Tribunal Court in this connection will be interesting. Tojo's answers to the prosecuting attorney's questions in regard to the fate of the flyers were as follows:

Q. The initial verdict was brought on the flyers as an instrument of threat to prevent further raids in Japan or in the Japanese occupied areas. Is this true?

A. Correct. It was for that reason. It was demanded by the General Headquarters. The Chief of the General Staff himself came directly to me to demand a severe punishment for the flyers. He was definitely in favor of the death penalty.

Q. Who was the Chief of the General Staff?

A. He was General Sugiyama.

Q. How did you reply to him? And to what extent did you settle the matter?

A. I agreed and ordered it even to that extent. It was the order directed to the military government. I do not know whether the order was issued in my name or General Headquarters, but at any rate, it was my responsibility.

General Sugiyama's strategy seems to have been to threaten whoever attempted to undertake such aerial attacks in the future. Heated debates took place between the Army General Headquarters and the Military Police Headquarters over questions that arose and particularly how and where the real trial should be held.

During those days when the prisoners were being played back and forth like pawns in a great chess game, they were constantly undergoing indignities, ill treatment, and torture.

The Japanese wanted to find out where the Americans had stored gasoline in China. On one occasion DeShazer was put on his knees and beaten severely. This brought no information. He was not an officer; consequently he had not been given such information. All he could say was that he did not know.

Some of the officers were treated even more roughly than DeShazer. Lieutenant Nielson, navigator from the other plane, was handcuffed and his hands lifted over his head to a peg on the wall. His toes just barely touched the floor. He was stretched out that way for about eight hours. Some of the other men were stretched out on boards. Towels were placed over their faces and water was poured over their noses and mouths. They would nearly suffocate. About all DeShazer can say about it now is, "It was very painful."

In the War Crimes Court in Tokyo, a statement was made to the effect that the eight American flyers were "the unfortunate victims of war." Speaking of the various types of treatment which the flyers received during this period, Lieutenant Nielson testified at the court of Shanghai at the conclusion of the war as follows:

Q. You state that you were kicked. Where were you kicked?

A. My leg.

Q. Who kicked it?

A. A Japanese military police.

Q. How hard did he kick it?

A. He kicked me so hard that he even left a scar.

Q. By applying this sort of treatment what did he attempt to secure?

A. They wanted to know the place from where we flew.

Q. Did you receive any ill treatment during the first night at Tokyo? If you did, what kind of treatment?

A. I was slapped on my head and face and was kicked on my leg.

Q. How were you bound?

A. My arms were bound to the back of the chair and my legs to the chair.

Q. About how many people participated in the inquiry?

A. Three military police, one interpreter, and one recorder.

Q. Where did they kick and slap?

A. They slapped my head and face and kicked my legs so hard that the wound which was received at the Shanghai prison re-opened and bled.

Q. What kind of questions were you asked?

A. The source of our flight. The question whether we bombed Tokyo during the previous week or not. A question as to our station prior to the Tokyo raid and whether we were real American soldiers.

Q. How long did the inquisition last?

A. Until four o'clock in the morning.

Q. During this period of time did they continue to mistreat you?

A. Yes. I was almost continuously beaten and kicked.

Q. During the eighteen days of inquisition, were you permitted to shave or take a bath?

A. No.

This type of questioning and treatment continued for approximately two months. A memorandum found in the diary of the Minister of the Imperial Household, Mr. Kido, dated May 21, states: "Some military leaders came into my office to discuss the punishment of the captive flyers." Obviously, the matter had been reported to the Imperial Court officials. Whether the Emperor had taken a hand in the matter at this time or not, the record does not show. In any event the Japanese Army Headquarters in Tokyo finally decided to have the men tried by a court martial under the 13th Army at Shanghai.

CHAPTER VI

DEATH SENTENCE COMMUTED BY EMPEROR HIROHITO

The return of the prisoners from Tokyo to Shanghai was not by airplane in a few hours as they had come over some two months before. Instead they went first by train to Nagasaki where they stayed for a night. Throughout this train trip they were handcuffed, legcuffed, and rope tied. They had not had opportunity to bathe for sixty days. The only chance even to wash their faces was a time or two with a little tea water. Under these conditions one can imagine how they must have appeared not having shaved during the entire two months. De-Shazer says concerning this train trip, "The coal soot from the train ride made us look as though we had been living in a pig sty."

At Nagasaki they were pushed into a prison cell whose walls were rough cold cement. There were a few Tatami (straw mats) on the floor. The stench from the toilet in the corner of the little room was revolting. After a while one of the guards came and put something in the toilet box to stop the awful smell. In spite of the unbearable conditions, the terrible surroundings, and the fact that they were already suffering from dysentery, the captured flyers found some joy in this prison experience in Nagasaki. For the first time since they had been captured, they were able to be together and talk with one another without interference from the guards. The five men from plane No. 16, of course, had been able to talk

some together, but as yet they did not know the story
concerning the three other men.

DeShazer admits they almost forgot the filth and dirt
while he and his four comrades from plane No. 16 listened to the thrilling story of the three men from plane
No. 6. The pilot of plane No. 6 was Lieutenant Dean
Hallmark from Texas; the co-pilot, Lieutenant Robert
Meder from Ohio; the navigator, Lieutenant C. T. Nielson. The bombardier and the rear gunner had been lost
in the crash landing at sea. Here is the story:

The plane ran out of gasoline just as it reached the
China coast. Lieutenant Hallmark tried to gain altitude
and fly over the mountains, but the airplane engine
finally sputtered and died. They made a crash landing
in the ocean and then found that their rubber life raft
was no good. Thinking that the plane would sink immediately, all five men jumped into the water and started
for the shore.

The bombardier and the rear gunner seemed to be
having trouble. Lieutenant Meder came back and tried
to help the rear gunner. Lieutenant Hallmark and Lieutenant Nielson were not aware that any of the men were
having difficulty. The water was icy cold and they were
far from shore.

Lieutenant Meder was a true soldier and a courageous
soul. He did his best to help the rear gunner, who evidently had been injured in the crash landing. With almost unbelievable courage and endurance, Lieutenant
Meder held on to his mate and swam in the icy water
until dawn. It seemed that Meder could not let go although his comrade had become entirely unconscious.
His frame was entirely limp. Undoubtedly, he was life-
less. Lieutenant Meder was finally able to reach the shore

with the body of his friend. Meder was completely exhausted. He collapsed on the beach, hardly out of reach of the water. In time, however, he revived somewhat and gained enough strength to climb farther up the beach. There to his amazement he saw the body of the bombardier lying on the sand. The tide had already brought him to shore faster than Meder himself had been able to swim with the limp form of the gunner. With all the strength he could gather, he tried to revive both men, but it was too late.

Thus there were only three survivors of plane No. 6. The men were not together when they reached the beach. Each one had to follow his best judgment. When Lieutenant Nielson reached the beach, he tried to crawl up the bank and seek some shelter and warmth. Suddenly, he felt himself falling. When he came to, it was daylight. He had fallen into a small canyon. He soon found a path and followed this until he came to a small village.

Lieutenant Hallmark had remained on the beach until daylight and then began looking around to get his bearings. He, too, found a path and walked into a village. To see an American soldier was an unusual sight, and he was quickly surrounded by Chinese soldiers. They took him to a small mud house and gave him some tea. Some of the Chinese tried to talk to him, but he could not understand them. Finally, one of the Chinese indicated that someone was coming. Lieutenant Hallmark thought that the Chinese were trying to warn him that the Japanese were coming to capture him. He picked up a large club and stood by the door with the club over his head. The door opened, and Lieutenant Nielson walked into the room. What a meeting! Although only

a few hours' time had elapsed since they had been together, the experiences through which they had gone
made it seem as if days had elapsed.

In due time, Lieutenant Meder was discovered by the
Chinese, and all three were brought together. The Chinese seemed to be gracious and gave them food. Referring to their description of this experience at a later
time, DeShazer says:

> It must have been fairly good food, for many times
> when hunger pangs were upon us, months later, we would
> hear these three refer to the food which they had eaten
> on this occasion.

The Chinese soldiers acted as if they were going to
help the airmen evade the Japanese. Great was their disappointment, when these very Chinese soldiers turned
them over to Japanese officials. They were then taken
to Shanghai and later flown to Tokyo. Now all eight
were together in the same prison cell at Nagasaki.

To their great relief, they spent but one night in this
awful prison. The surroundings were almost unendur-
able. They were sick in body; yet to their real satisfaction they had had opportunity to talk together. Obviously, there had been little sleep. The next morning
they were put on a ship which took them, still handcuffed and tied, back to Shanghai. They arrived on June
19, 1942. The previous sixty days had been like a nightmare, but the next seventy days were to be days of stark
horror.

As soon as the captives landed in Shanghai, they were
taken immediately to the "Bridge House." They were in
poor physical condition, greatly emaciated and barely
able to move.

They were placed in a prison cell with fifteen Chinese prisoners, two of whom were women. The size of the cell was twelve by fifteen feet. An open box was used as a receptacle.

Food consisted of a cup of boiled rice soup for breakfast, four ounces of bread for lunch and four ounces of bread again for dinner. Approximately two quarts of water were given per day to the eight Americans. Lieutenant Hallmark was on a stretcher, but the other seven men, though considerably weakened, were able to stand.

Most of the other prisoners were covered with scabs and old sores. They were very weak and made a most pitiful appearance. The room being so small, there was not enough space for all to lie down at one time. Bedbugs, lice, and large rats were plentiful. It was now midsummer in 1942. The weather was hot and the water available was inadequate. DeShazer in telling about the situation makes rather revealing and philosophical observations:

> One day one of the Chinese women fell down and hurt her head. They laughed and said she was pretending to be sick. Guards hit her on the head with a stick, which was attached to their keys. They seemed to be the very lowest type of people. Sometimes they would make us stand up during the night after they had awakened us from our sleep. They would threaten to hit us with long clubs which they poked through the bars of the cell.
>
> It was the first time that I had ever been in such a wicked environment. I could not help wondering why there was so much difference between America and the Orient. There is bad in America, but the bad in America does not begin to compare with that which we observed. The truth was beginning to dawn upon me—it is Christianity that makes the difference. Even though many people in America do not profess to be Christians, yet they

are following the Christian ways. Even the non-Christian people in America do not hit women over the head. The people who are Christians have shown the rest of the world the right way to act. It is because God has said Christians are to be the light of the world. I had always tried to steer away from religion, but now I was beginning to see that Christianity is a great benefit to mankind. It is God's plan for mankind's happiness.

In the daytime we were supposed to sit straight up on the floor without any support for our backs. Often the guards would catch us leaning back on our elbows. There was always a quarrel as soon as we were caught. The guard would try to hit us on the head with a bamboo stick. The Chinese prisoners would allow themselves to be beaten and would then thank the Japanese guards. We always tried to talk the guards out of the notion of hitting us, but sometimes we would have to take the punishment.

One day the guard caught Lieutenant Hite and Lieutenant Farrow leaning against the wall. He hollered, "Kurah" (Hey!) and opened the door. His sword and steel scabbard were used to hit them on the head. Lieutenant Hite grabbed the weapon, and the guard pulled his sword out of the scabbard. It looked as if Hite was going to be killed, but the guard finally calmed down and acted more human.

We weren't getting much food. Lieutenant Hallmark was a large man. His frame needed something to fill it up. We were all weak from the lack of water and food. One day Lieutenant Hallmark passed out. He was very sick after that. We had to carry him to the toilet. He had dysentery, and we had to take him about every fifteen minutes. We had regular shifts, but it was too hard on us; finally, all of us gave out. We were all lying flat on our backs from exhaustion and practically ready to give up.

Such was the situation and the condition under which these American boys lived for seventy long days. Along with the sickness, filth, and constant brutality was the ever-present suspense regarding what the Japanese government was going to do with them. Rumors were frequent that they were to be executed. From time to time they were subjected to further questionings. Whatever remained of morale was scarcely perceptible. They were dejected, discouraged, and almost hopeless.

At one period during those dark days they were taken before Major-General Shoji Ito, Chief Justice Officer of the Japanese 13th Army Military Court at Shanghai. We now know that this was the official court-martial for the American flyers. The trial took place at the tribunal courthouse, headed by a prosecutor, Major Itsura Hata. The judges were Yamitsu, Okada, and Tatsuta. Lieutenant Hallmark had to be carried to the court on a stretcher, but the rest of the defendants stood during the trial.

There was no defense attorney, nor was there any statement declaring innocence or guilt. There was no witness. The trial could scarcely be called one of justice, for the Tokyo Headquarters had already decided the fate of the prisoners. Personal word was brought from Tokyo by Colonel Arisue. He reported that General Sugiyama expected the death penalty for each member of the group.

During the trial the prosecutor, Hata, gave the names of the eight prisoners and then proceeded to state the evidences of the "indiscriminate bombing" during the Doolittle raid over Japanese cities. He reported that in these raids non-military people had been killed. He also declared that the bombings were against the military laws; therefore all of the flyers who participated in this offense would receive the death sentence.

At the conclusion of the trial, the judges condemned all eight of the Americans to be executed. The verdict was promptly relayed to Tokyo. The American airmen, of course, were not informed.

General Sugiyama thought the death sentence was proper. There were many, however, in the department of the Japanese Army and in the army of occupation in Shanghai, who felt that the punishment was stricter than necessary. This idea was undoubtedly due to the fact that the war had just begun and the people as yet were not as war-minded as later on. At that time the punishment seemed too severe. The people's attitude in this regard toward the end of the war would certainly have been different, for by that time hatred against the victorious Americans had mounted. Many weeks passed by as the matter was being given final consideration at the Tokyo Headquarters.

In the meantime conditions in the prison at the "Bridge House" and the health of the prisoners had reached the point where it was absolutely necessary to improve the situation if the prisoners were to continue to live at all. So it was that after they had spent seventy days in the twelve by fifteen cell, the prisoners were taken out and moved to another prison just outside Shanghai. Lieutenant Hallmark was wrapped in a blanket and laid on the floor. Again they were all taken before some Japanese Army officials to answer questions and tell about their past history.

In this new prison solitary confinement began in earnest. Each man was placed in a small cell about nine by five feet. The conditions were materially better than in the previous prison, but at the same time there was still the haunting fear, both throughout the day and during the long nights, that at any time they might be called out to face a firing squad or something worse.

During these days among the Tokyo officials some interesting things were happening. Jealousies and rivalries between top Army leaders and officials in the War Cabinet flared up and played a part in the final decision regarding the sentence of death on the American flyers. According to the records, we now know that the incident had been reported to the Imperial Court family. The record of the Minister of the Imperial Household states that on October 3, 1942,

> Premier Tojo came in at 11:30. He gave a detailed account of the capture of the flyers and the proposed punishment. I was requested to report it to the Emperor. I was given an audience by the Emperor from 1:05 to 1:15 P.M. and related Tojo's message to him.

The record further shows that Kido, the Minister of the Imperial Household, told the Emperor that Tojo was in favor of a more lenient punishment, but that a formal decision of the death penalty for all the flyers had been made by a responsible authority, General Sugiyama, Chief of the General Staff.

In the international Military Tribunal which was held in Tokyo following the close of the War, testimony was given which shows that there was considerable rivalry between General Sugiyama and General Tojo in this connection. It seems that each General was trying to get an audience with the Emperor in advance of the other. Had General Sugiyama* been able to have talked with the Emperor first, undoubtedly all the prisoners would have been executed. Tojo, however, was able to reach the Emperor first and make a request for leniency before Sugiyama had made a formal demand for the

---

* Sugiyama committed suicide on the day Japan surrendered.

death penalty. He continued his insistence that the Americans were criminals.

Some of the questions and answers which appear on the record of the International Military Tribunal regarding this matter, though somewhat difficult to understand, will be of interest. The questions were put to General Tojo* by an Allied prosecutor:

Q. When General Sugiyama requested the death sentence for the flyers, did he come to you as a representative of someone in the Imperial Headquarters?

A. No. He did not represent anyone. He came along on his own initiative. Since the Chief of the General Staff had seldom shown up by himself, I can remember the incident very well.

Q. Have you ever discussed his order with the Emperor?

A. No. The Emperor did not enter into this matter. The reports from the court-martial which took place in China showed that General Sugiyama had asked for a verdict of death for all eight flyers. The Chief of the General Staff came to me demanding that the decision be carried out without failure. However, since I had known of the humane nature of the Emperor, it would be to his wish that the death penalty be applied to the smallest possible number of prisoners. For this reason only the three who had killed a school child were to receive the death sentence. I consulted the Emperor regarding this matter, for he was the only authority who could issue the reduction of the sentence. This is the only point which was called to the Emperor's attention.

---

* General Tojo was executed by the Allied military authorities following this trial.

Q. In other words the Emperor re-examined the issue and reduced the death penalty of the eight flyers to three, did he not?

A. No. He did not re-examine the issue. In Japan the decision made by the court-martial cannot be re-examined and changed.

Q. What made the Emperor decide this way? Was it because of your suggestion?

A. Yes. His advisers usually discussed issues of importance with him. However, it was the Emperor who reduced the sentence. He was very generous.

Q. After a long discussion of the verdict, Sugiyama went to the Palace and was informed that the Emperor had commuted the sentence. Thereupon, Sugiyama wired General Hata, Commanding General in occupied China, as follows: "I believe the verdict issued by the Chief prosecutor at the military tribunal was fair. However, I am convinced that the sentence for the flyers should be commuted, except for three flyers. The others will receive life sentences. Lieutenant Colonel Takayama will be dispatched from Fukukoka on the thirteenth of this month (October) to carry out the punishment. All questions should be directed to him."

A further message was sent from General Sugiyama listing the names of the flyers sentenced to death: Pilot Hallmark, Pilot Farrow and machine gunner Spaatz; those commuted to life sentence: Meder, Nielson, Hite, Barr, DeShazer. This message further revealed that the death sentence was to be carried out October 15. The record does not show whether the executions were carried out on this particular date or not. The testimony in the Allied War Trials indicates that it was about that date when the three unfortunate Americans were shot, either in the outskirts of Shanghai or in a military prison yard late at night in secrecy.

Those who were condemned to life imprisonment were deprived of the privilege of prisoner's exchange. From that time on they were not given the normal treatment received by other prisoners of war.

Of course, these military conferences and discussions were going on, wholly unknown to the American flyers. About the middle of October, when for some time they had been in solitary confinement in individual cells and yet able to be with each other a few minutes each day, suddenly they found that three of the men did not appear. From that time on they were seen no more. The other five did not know what had happened to the three until they gained their freedom after the close of the war.

Soon after the disappearance of three of the men, the remaining five were taken into a court room. Knowing that three of their companions had disappeared, they were naturally worried concerning this particular move. While they were standing before the judge, he read off a long statement in Japanese. When it was interpreted, they learned that they were to receive life imprisonment with "special treatment." They were told that they had been sentenced to be executed but that the Emperor of Japan had changed the order and they were to receive life imprisonment. Following this statement they were taken back to their cells—to ponder and ponder and ponder! Speaking concerning this particular experience, DeShazer says:

> I had expected to be executed from the way the Japanese had acted. It was really a relief to know that they were now planning to let us remain alive. I could not help feeling a strange sense of joy, even though solitary

confinement and a long war awaited any possible chance of freedom. At the same time it seemed almost hopeless to think of ever being free again, since the most probable thing would be that we would be executed when America did win the war.

CHAPTER VII

SEASON AFTER SEASON IN SOLITARY CONFINEMENT

DeShazer and his four companions, not knowing what had happened to their three comrades but realizing they themselves had escaped execution for the time being at least, began to think more of their immediate future. It was now just six months since they had taken off the *Hornet* amidst the cheers of thousands of American soldiers and sailors. During the six-month period they had come to know something of suffering, fear, and almost death.

Now as they looked to the future with the thought of solitary confinement and perhaps a long war, a spirit of hopelessness again took possession of them. Each was in a little cell nine by five feet with no window except a small opening near the ceiling. Guards were in front of the door. There were no books, no radios, no newspapers, no play, no fellowship. Since their sentence included "special treatment" it meant no letters to or from home and no Red Cross packages. In this regard the situation was entirely different from an internment camp.

They remembered something of what the hot summer of 1942 had been. Now it was late October and winter not far away. Had they known at that time there would be no heat in the prison, even during the coldest, freezing winter weather, their spirits would have dropped even lower if that could have been possible.

As the days came and went, however, sheer necessity

required that they adjust to the situation. They tried their best to fraternize with the guards. They were particularly anxious to find what had happened to their three companions. For a few minutes each morning, they were allowed to get out of their cells in order to wash their hands and brush their teeth. Occasionally, a guard or an official would come and take them out for a little exercise.

One morning when they were taking exercises under the direction of the head official, Lieutenant Hite asked this man what had happened to the three men who had been taken away. The guard's interpreter, who was himself a prisoner, said that the official told him they had been taken to another prison camp. In the further conversation the interpreter got his words mixed and for a moment had the men aghast. The interpreter, who was really trying to befriend the Americans, told them that "they were going to all be executed." Under the shock of this statement, their faces showed how startled they were and they also demonstrated their interest in looking for ways and means of escaping from the prison. Upon realizing his error, the interpreter said he was sorry and explained he had made a mistake. What he was trying to say was that they were to have been executed but had been granted mercy by the Emperor. This statement further confirmed them in their belief that the announcement of the Japanese judge was correct in regard to their sentence to be executed having been commuted to life imprisonment. For many weeks this interpreter was a source of encouragement. He was half Japanese and half Portuguese.

The many weary hours spent in solitary confinement made it difficult to think normally. There was the con-

stant problem of how to occupy their minds. By yelling
they could hear one another from one cell to another.
Yelling, however, attracted the guards and brought reprimand and punishment. At one time during a period of
six or eight weeks they made somewhat of a game of their
meager food rations. They worked out a little scheme
of drawing numbers so one day a week the fellow who
drew the winning number would receive from each of
the others an extra half bowl of rice or a bowl of soup.
Lieutenant Meder seems to have been the instigator of
the idea. By a mere coincidence it seems that he lost
more than anyone else. DeShazer rather boasted of the
fact that he seemed to win more times than any of the
others. Commenting on this DeShazer says:

> We had lots of fun over this game, although it only
> lasted for about two months and even then only once a
> week. We often used to agree in advance to trade a bowl
> of rice for two bowls of soup. When the food came, how-
> ever, we would howl and complain about the other fellow
> being a sharp trader if we thought he got the best of the
> deal. We never knew, of course, in advance what the food
> was going to be, but it kept us amused to trade around
> with one another.

It seems that throughout the rest of their imprisonment, DeShazer had fun poked at him from time to time
for having been such a winner in this period of trading
food.

Another and almost unbelievable activity engaged in
by DeShazer in order to occupy his time was climbing
the walls of his cell. Since the cell was only five feet
wide, it was possible for him to put his hands on one
wall and his feet on the other. By proper maneuvering
he was able to climb in this fashion to the ceiling. It

was about a twelve-foot climb. When up near the ceiling, he could look out the little window and see the country side for miles around. Obviously, this was good exercise, and it was a real joy to look out on the scenery after the long hours of looking at four walls. Fortunately for him he was never caught in this act by any guard.

When winter came, DeShazer and his comrades were given some additional clothing, but still there was much suffering. Lieutenant Hite became very sick and suffered from the damp, cold cell. He was very sick for about three months. During this period he became erratic, both in his conversation and in his actions. He did not return to normal until early spring.

In April, 1943, practically one year after the fateful day of the Tokyo raid, DeShazer and his comrades were taken by airplane from Shanghai to Nanking. Such a move naturally aroused anticipation and a certain amount of excitement. They were particularly hoping for a nice courtyard outside the prison in which they would be free to move around. They felt that they had had their full share of solitary confinement. There was a perpetual dread in their minds of being all alone in a prison cell. There was also the dread of intense cold in the winter and extreme heat in the summer. But their hopes for relief were doomed to disappointment.

Immediately upon arriving in Nanking, they were again placed in solitary confinement. They did, however, find some relief in that occasionally the guards in the Nanking prison showed some friendship. Evidently, being a guard in a prison was itself a somewhat lonesome business. The guards, even though ordered not to give out information, did occasionally try to talk to the prisoners. It was through these conversations that the American boys were able to glean, from time to time, some scant information concerning what was going on in the war. By piecing together bits of such information they finally determined that the whole Japanese Navy had been sunk. At other times the guards would become abusive and cruel.

Each day for a few minutes DeShazer and his comrades were taken outside so their cells could be cleaned and also so the men could have a little exercise. It was during these brief moments of exercise that all five occasionally could get together. The guards would allow them to say as much as "Hello" to one another, but if they said much more the guards would usually yell, "Shut up!"

Hours were many and long. Days were long. Week after week came and went. The hot summer of 1943 finally passed and once again there was the comfort of fall.

Occasionally, things became a little brighter. Once in a while, a guard would allow the airmen during the exercise period to talk at length among themselves. At times the guards would themselves wrestle with the prisoners. They called it "smoe." The American men were considerably larger than their guards. In view of this the guards could not hold them down, but they were exceptionally good at kicking and tripping. Usually by this method they would finally get the Americans down. When this occurred, they immediately waved their handkerchiefs over their heads, said the match was over, and shouted, "Nippon benzai! Nippon benzai!" (Japan wins! Japan wins!)

The conversation of the guards concerning the war,

in general, however, implied that Japan was winning all the time. Frequently they told the Americans that there was no hope for them, that everything was going in Japan's favor. As a rule, during such a conversation, they would finally swing around and say, "Well, if Japan should lose and America should win, prisoners would not be set free. Instead, they would all have their heads cut off." They insisted that the Japanese expected to fight until the last man died, and of course, they said the Emperor of Japan would be the last one to die. Not once was a critical word spoken against the Emperor.

Through such conversations DeShazer and his comrades came to know more of the Japanese worship of their Emperor. The Japanese people believed the Emperor was the representative on earth of deity. They also believed their Emperor could not be wrong in any of his words or deeds. Since the Emperor had asked them to fight for their country, it was their highest honor and joy to do so and, if need be, to die. Referring to some of these conversations and particularly the slant the Japanese had concerning the war, DeShazer says:

> They would tell us many fantastic tales of how God was on their side and how they were able to sink many ships with just one airplane. It seemed to be their belief that they were in the right as far as the war was concerned. They said that America had started the war. We were greatly surprised when they brought out some of their arguments. It seemed hard to understand how grown men could believe some of the things the Japanese government was telling their people. However, these men were convinced that they were in the right and that their country was going to win. They had a confidence in a supernatural power that was unshakable. These bloody Chinese head-removers said that they were in the right and that God was always on the side of righteousness.

Moralizing on the situation, DeShazer says further:

These men had never been taught about the true God.
How could they know that the God who has been revealed for all mankind is on the side of peace. They did
not know about Jesus who died on the cross to pay the
penalty for the sin of hatred and the lust for power.
They did not know about the Spirit of Jesus that will
enter into a person and take away the hatred and greed
of this world. They had only been taught about a god
who was seeking everything for Japan. They needed to
know about Jesus who was God's true representative for
every nation and every generation of men.

Just about the time of the fall equinox in 1943, Lieutenant Meder took very sick with dysentery. His comrades had noticed for some time that he was looking increasingly thin and weak. One day all five were in the
yard together. It was a beautiful fall day, and they were
allowed to run about a little. Lieutenant Meder was able
to be up and out but was not able to exercise. Those who
were able to run around the yard together, naturally
would whisper to one another and exchange information concerning what they had been able to pry out of
the guards. They were always very solicitous concerning
each other's opinions as to how each felt. There was
always the constant fear of disease taking hold on them
or of their losing their mental faculties.

On this particular day they were all anxious about
Meder, but they did not dare to stop and gather around
him and make inquiry. Lieutenant Nielson, however,
went to Meder and asked him how he was feeling. Several guards were in the yard, but one particular guard
seemed to have charge of the exercise for this day. When
this guard saw Nielson over at the side of the yard talking
to Meder, he yelled at him, "Shut up!" Nielson paid no

attention to the guard; this seemed to make him very angry. For a time the guard muttered and swore. De-Shazer and the other airmen were soon required to stop running around, pick up the pails and tools which they had been using to clean the cells, and return to their cells. Once again the guard yelled at Nielson and Meder who were making the most of their time together by talking as fast as they could. Neither of the officers for a time paid any attention to the guard. When Nielson finally came up to where the guard was standing, the guard reached out and slapped Nielson's face. Lieutenant Nielson calmly set his bucket down on the ground. He cleared his throat—"Ahem." Then, slowly, without any trace of anger, Nielson reached out and slapped the guard's face.

Everyone was shocked. No one knew what would happen next. Seven or eight guards had come into the yard to watch the men exercise. They all sucked air through their teeth as the Japanese do when they see something which surprises them. The guard who was slapped was humiliated and, of course, very angry. He started to strike Nielson with his steel scabbard, but Nielson was an expert in getting out of the way. De-Shazer says:

> It was comical to see the way Nielson dodged the blows of the angry guard. One swing would have killed him if the guard could have made contact. One of the guards who had been watching tried to stop the fight and was rewarded for his good intentions by the swinging scabbard hitting the back of his hand. After that the fight ended.

All the men were then put back in their cells. Nielson, of course, as well as the others wondered what the penalty would be. Prisoners held by the Japanese had been beheaded for no greater breach than had been committed by Nielson. To the surprise of everyone, however, the whole affair was never mentioned again. It seems that most of the guards even admired Nielson for his courage.

Weeks went by. Lieutenant Meder continued to grow worse, and died December 1. No one will ever know all the thoughts of this man who had spent many lonely hours in suffering in that far-off prison cell. His comrades fain would have helped him but this, of course, was out of the question. He held the highest esteem of his comrades. It was Meder who had tried to rescue two of his comrades after the crash landing at the close of that fateful day after leaving the aircraft carrier, *Hornet*. In speaking of him DeShazer says:

> Lieutenant Meder seemed to understand the Bible message well. He and I had a good talk one day while we were pulling weeds out in the yard. Meder told me that Jesus Christ is the Lord and coming King, that Jesus is God's Son and that God expects the nations and the people to recognize Jesus as Lord and Saviour. He said that the war would last until Jesus Christ caused it to stop. I did not understand what he meant at the time, but I remembered his words later. Lieutenant Meder had a very brilliant mind. He was truly a gentleman in every way, and he was a prince of a fellow.

Meder's comrades, however, did not know immediately of his death. Suddenly they were aware of considerable hammering out in the yard. DeShazer crawled up and peeked out the window. He saw they were making a large box. The next day DeShazer and the other three airmen, one at a time, were taken from their cells around into Meder's cell where they could take a last look. He was lying in the box with a nice wreath of flowers and a copy of the Bible on the lid of the box. A short time after when they were back in their cells, they could tell by the sounds that the box with their comrade's body was being carried out. Later a small box was brought back, which the guard said contained the ashes of Lieutenant Meder.

Evidently the death of Lieutenant Meder, when reported to the "higher ups" in the military government in Japan, brought about reprimands and a change in procedure. In a few days the captain of the prison came in to talk to the prisoners and try to cheer them. He even went so far as to ask what they would like to have. They responded immediately that they would like to have some bread, butter, jam, steak, eggs, milk, and other kinds of American food. They knew, of course, that no Japanese official could provide such food, but almost twenty months on rations in an Oriental prison made them have an indescribable longing for American food.

To their delight the Japanese official did arrange for them to be given bread with their daily ration of rice and soup. He also made arrangements for them to be fed three times, rather than twice each day. This was one of the most outstanding events during the winter of 1943-44. Soon both their health and their spirits greatly improved.

The airmen had also hoped in this new arrangement to have a change in conditions so that they could hear from home. There had been no word from America. This continued to be denied. But they were provided with a few books to read. How fortunate it was that among these books was a Bible—an American Standard Edition. DeShazer was the only man in the group who was not an officer. This meant that the other three men, being officers, had first choice with respect to reading. Not until the beginning of summer did DeShazer have the

privilege of having the Bible. Even then it was his privilege for only three weeks.

Prior to the time DeShazer obtained the Bible he had
the great pleasure of getting one or two other books. He
made use of his time in memorizing portions from these
books as indicated in a letter to the author by Captain C.
J. Nielson. In describing the long weary hours in solitary
confinement Nielson referred to the "gnawing hunger in
our heads and stomachs." He indicates that each of the
men resorted to different things in an effort to occupy his
mind. He says:

> During those many hours and months I tried by mental
> pictures to plan a home. Lieutenant Barr was working on
> an elaborate neon sign, and Lieutenant Hite tried to plan
> a model farm. Meanwhile DeShazer was memorizing a
> very long poem, "The Pleasures of Hope," from one of the
> few books we were able to have. He would recite parts of
> it to us when we came together for our recreational period
> and we all learned various portions. Some of these lines
> will stay with me forever, such as
>
> > Lo, Nature, Life and Liberty illume
> > The dim-eyed tenant of the dungeon gloom.
> > Truth shall pervade the unfathomed darkness there,
> > And light the dreadful features of despair.

Captain Nielson also states that he found many new
things in the Bible while reading it over and over during
the days the copy was in his possession.

1. MacArthur's Headquarters — the Dai Ichi Building

2. Famous Torii.

1. Highway along beach — Mt. Fuji in background

2. Japanese women on picnic.

Tokyo Today

This view of a side street in Tokyo shows trend to western architecture and clothing.

1. Fishermen's Houses.

2. Yokohama City Center.

1. Oxcart at Yokasuka.

2. Women carrying seaweed.

Rural Scene in Japan
A land of intense cultivation where 81,500,000 people live in area size of California.

CHAPTER VIII

HAS BIBLE FOR THREE PRECIOUS WEEKS

Only eternity will reveal exactly what happened in a little prison cell in far off Nanking, China, sometime in May, 1944. The exact day is not known, but a most significant event took place. There sat DeShazer in solitary confinement hour after hour, day after day. He was homesick, hungry, discouraged, and almost hopeless. Throughout the dreary weeks of more than two long years, he had been waiting, waiting—and thinking. Recreation had been meager. The privilege of reading was almost unknown. His comrades, however, had been telling him about the copy of the Bible which they had been reading. Then one day it came his turn.

The Bible—that was the Book he had heard read at the family altar in that little rural home just outside Madras, Oregon, years before. That was the Book from which lessons had been studied in the Sunday school in the modest little Free Methodist Church and the Methodist Episcopal Church in that same isolated village. That was the Book he had long since lost interest in—if, in truth, he had ever had interest in it—until after many months in prison.

Now it was his turn to have the Bible. It was laid in his hands. Who brought it to the prison he will never know—whether Protestant or Catholic, it does not matter. With almost feverish grasp he seized the Bible and pressed it to his bosom.

Yes, the Bible, the very Word of God! The Book of

books which has been the inspiration of the lives of multiplied thousands. From the cultural and aesthetic point of view the Bible has been the inspiration of poets, artists, musicians, orators, sculptors, authors, and many others throughout the centuries. Then, too, it has been the silent inspiration of millions of people entirely lost in the masses but devout followers of Jesus Christ who have poured over its pages and received personal encouragement, comfort, and strength. This was the Book which fell into DeShazer's hands. Yes, the "best seller" according to the records of the publishers, but in a cold dingy prison cell, unknown to the most of the world, the Bible became the *best read* Book to this young man.

The light in DeShazer's cell was horribly dim, and the print was fairly small, but that did not matter. He opened the Book and began to read. From then on there was little time for sleep. He had been warned that he could have the Book only three weeks. He read and read and read! He read the entire Book through several times. He read the Prophets through six times. Many hours were spent in memorizing. The entire Bible seemed to become alive. It appeared to be illuminated. Certain passages seemed to blaze forth with mysterious brightness. Certainly, here was evidence of a profound truth, "the Word has power." We also see clear evidence of the faithful working of the Holy Spirit. DeShazer had no one to guide him such as a pastor, a Sunday-school worker, a teacher, or a friend. But the Comforter, who was sent into the world to guide into all truth, was present to guide this spiritually hungry young man.

Trying to relive those wonderful days, DeShazer has tried to put into words the thoughts which came to his mind. Without doubt, what he has written has been influenced by his study and experiences since being set free. At the same time it is most interesting to review what DeShazer himself feels were his conclusions as he read and reread the Bible during those memorable three weeks, and then more than twelve months afterwards in solitary confinement as he tried to recapture the words of precious memory:

The Bible is different from any other Book which has been written. The men who wrote the Bible said that God spoke to them and it has proved that God did speak to them. These men wrote down what God revealed to them. The prophets foretold the greatest event that ever happened in the history of mankind. They foretold the coming of God's Son, Jesus Christ, the Saviour for all the people in the world.

Other books which have been written do not make the claim that God spoke to their authors. They couldn't prove that God spoke to them if they did not make such a claim. The Bible has proof that God did speak to the Bible writers. The events which they proclaimed came to pass—even the event of Deity coming to our world was known to these men. Since God spoke to them, we know that the Bible is true. It contains God's word. It is God's plan for our salvation and not man's. The supernatural power that created this world has given a revelation to all mankind so that we can know the truth. God has revealed His power through the manifestation of the universe. He has spoken to mankind and given them his law. The Bible is not man's reasoning. It is God's Word.

As I read the prophets through over and over again I was amazed at the way they could foretell such a great event as the coming of the Son of God. They were able to know that the one who created this world was going to be born into this world as a little baby. The men of the Old Testament times agreed with the men of the New Testament times. We are all sinners and all in need of a Saviour. This Saviour was to die on the cross according to the prophets, and the New Testament writers told how this prophecy had been fulfilled in Jesus. The death on the cross paid the penalty for all sins. Jesus saved us from the penalty of death. His death satisfied the law of God which says that a soul that sins will surely die. The penalty of God's law having been paid God can now legally pardon a sinner while he still maintains justice. The many writers of the Bible agree to this one central plan of redemption.

God spoke to Abraham, the first Jew, and told him that God would make a great nation of his children. In the years that followed the Jewish nation was formed. About four hundred years after Abraham, Moses became the leader of the Jewish nation. Moses lived about one thousand five hundred years before Jesus Christ. But even though the Messiah was so many years after Moses, the great prophet Moses knew about His coming. The Jewish people were God's chosen people. This statement was made by God to the Jewish prophets. God made a great nation of the Jewish people, leading them in miraculous ways and delivering them from their enemies by mysterious powers which God alone knows how to use.

The prophets could tell many events which were going to come to pass in the near future and in the ages to come. This was a sign to those people in that time that God spoke to the prophets who could foretell the future. The people respected the prophets. They were men with whom God spoke, and they told the people what God's law is.

The Jewish people made sacrifices of cattle, sheep, goats, and fowls for the purpose of making atonement for their sins. The prophets told the people that we have all sinned. Every person does something which is wrong. God made us to be perfect, but, because man had fallen from the perfect state in which God made him, we are all imperfect. Imperfection is no glory to God. Our imperfection is displeasing to God.

However, God is willing to forgive us if we have faith in Him. To show that they had faith in God, the Jewish people made sacrifices for an atonement for their sins. Of course, the prophets knew that these sacrifices of animals would never satisfy the law of God which says that the person must die if he sins. However, the prophets knew that the death of God's Son would make an atonement for all sins which were ever committed in this world if people showed that they had faith to believe God. The sacrifice of animals was the means which God had given to the Jewish people of the Old Testament age for a sign of their faith. Some of the Jewish prophets saw the salvation plan of God clearly. To some of the people God revealed just enough for them at that particular time.

As DeShazer continued to read his Bible and study, such truths and conclusions as the foregoing were constantly coming to mind. For many years he had been careless, indifferent, and skeptical. As he continued to read the Bible, new truths seemed to be staring at him. Increasingly he began looking for proof of the existence of God and his revelation to human beings. As he was reading Isaiah, for instance, and thinking about the time which was hundreds of years before Christ, he came to this verse: "Surely he hath borne our griefs and carried our sorrows: yet we did esteem him stricken, smitten of God, and afflicted. But he was wounded for our transgressions, he was bruised for our iniquities: the chastisement of our peace was upon him; and with his stripes we are healed. All we like sheep have gone astray; we have turned every one to his own way; and the Lord hath laid on him the iniquity of us all" (Isa. 53:5-6).

DeShazer began to see how the prophecies in the Old Testament were revealed in the New. He became enamored with the sense of the supernatural. Having read the prophecy in Isaiah, he says he was greatly impressed when he came to the twenty-seventh chapter of Matthew and read how the people seeing Jesus on the Cross, as Isaiah had prophesied, "esteemed him stricken, smitten of God and afflicted." They "reviled him, wagging their heads." They said, "He trusted in God; let hin. 'eliver him now, if he will have him: for he said, I am the Son of God" (Matt. 27:43). DeShazer seemed to put himself in the place of the Jews, and he felt he could understand Jesus' hanging on the cross was sure proof that Jesus was indeed a fraud. From their point of view, God had forsaken the Christ and was using this means of punishing Him. Then DeShazer following the Gospel story realized how the resurrection of Jesus was a complete fulfillment of the prophecy which was found in the Old Testament.

The prophets had foretold what would take place. Daniel said, "Messiah shall be cut off" (Dan. 9:26). In Zech. 13:7 DeShazer read, "Smite the shepherd, and the sheep shall be scattered."

The perfect agreement between the writers of the Old Testament and the New was a revelation to this new student of the Bible. He was thinking:

> Yes, Christ died for us; that is the message all the way through the Bible. Many different people were writing, but the same revelation of salvation was given to every one. The same thread of thought is carried from Genesis to Revelation. I've seen proof of it in my lifetime. I've seen the handiwork of God. God has manifested Himself for us to see.

Along the same line he seemed to be charmed by the love of God:

> Jesus existed as God's Son before the world was created, but when the time was fulfilled God sent His Son into the world to take on the form of a human being. It

was nearly two thousand years ago that this great event happened. God had foretold this event through prophecy. Now God gave the sign of miracles which Jesus performed. Jesus also claimed to be the One who fulfilled prophecy. Now God, to make it sure that we could believe, raised Jesus from the dead. Jesus had died for us. We do not need to suffer the penalty for sin now. We do not need to die.

It is difficult for us in normal situations to grasp what was going on in the soul of this American prisoner as he tried to grasp the truth of the great Book. Over and over he would go back to the prophets and then come again to the New Testament. Hour after hour he read. One reference after another was followed through. Without doubt a miracle was taking place daily within his heart and mind. New insights were revealed. New passages were grasped:

God made it very plain that a Saviour was needed and that a Saviour was coming. As the prophets had foretold, the Saviour was born in Bethlehem. Jesus, the Saviour, lived in Bethlehem. Jesus, the Saviour, lived a sinless life. He performed many great miracles.

Jesus made it clear that He is the "Christ, the Son of the living God" (Matt. 16:16). He was the One the prophets had made so many statements about. Jesus told the people that He existed before Abraham, who had lived nearly two thousand years previously. In John 17:5, Jesus tells of the glory which He had with the Father before the world was created. Jesus boldly claimed to be God to which the Jewish people reacted by picking up stones to stone Him. When Jesus asked them the reason for their desire to stone Him, they said because of blasphemy and because He made out that He himself was God. (John 10:33.)

Some of the Jewish leaders became angry at Jesus' teachings. He was different from any other person that

had been in the world before. He is the only one that
could fill the position of the Messiah. There never will
be anyone else that can truthfully make the statements
that Jesus made; for instance, "I am the resurrection and
the life: he that believeth in me, though he were dead, yet
shall he live" (John 11:25). It must have been astounding blasphemy to many of the Jews to see a man stand up
and make such a claim.

A few of the Jewish leaders gathered together a mob
which caught Jesus and received permission to crucify
Him. Jesus was nailed to the cross as it was foretold in
prophecy. They drove nails through His hands and feet.
David had written about this in the twenty-second Psalm.
It was a shameful death that the wicked mob forced upon
Jesus. Two thieves were crucified with Him. The Roman
soldiers and the people made fun of Jesus and tortured
Him, but God allowed all this to happen to His Son that
people might be saved.

They took Jesus down from the cross, and three days
later Jesus arose from the grave and appeared to His
followers. They had searched for Him in the grave, but
they could not find Him. One day a short time after the
resurrection of Jesus, His disciples were in a room where
the windows were shut and the doors were all locked.
Jesus came into that room. He was supernatural. The
walls could not stop Him. Jesus showed His followers the
holes in His hands which the nails had caused when He
hung from the cross. He showed them the hole in His
side when they pierced Him with the spear while He was
on the cross. Jesus was showing Himself to His followers
to prove that He is "the resurrection and the life." He
showed Himself to over five hundred people at one time.
On one occasion Jesus was talking to His disciples and
while He was talking He was parted from them and taken
up into the sky. He disappeared in the clouds.

The light was shining brighter and brighter. Perhaps
the memory of boyhood days in Sunday school, long covered by the debris of careless thinking and worldly liv-

ing, was being revived, and truths long forgotten were returning to mind. We do not know. Certainly, the Spirit of God was making it possible for DeShazer—without the assistance of priest, minister, teacher, or friend—to get a theological course unprecedented in its scope and intensity. Certainly he was coming nearer to the inner revelation of God to himself.

As he continued to read and study as long as daylight would allow, his mind seemed to catch greater and greater truths:

> This is the greatest event that has happened in the history of mankind. It is of more importance to us than anything else. It is the only time that God has raised a man from the grave. Why was God so particular to raise Jesus from the grave? Why did God single Him out of all the millions of people? Obviously, the reason is that Christ was the Son of God.
>
> God put His seal on Jesus Christ through the sign of prophecy and through the sign of the resurrection from the dead. Both of these facts agree. God has scientifically proved to all mankind that Jesus Christ is our Saviour. Anyone who can read can search out the Messiah. He boldly stands out from all others. The Bible is a wonderful Book!
>
> There is no reason for me to doubt the fact of the resurrection of Jesus. The men relating the events which took place gave us truthful accounts. They were men who wouldn't tell a lie. They believed that liars would receive punishment in hell's fire throughout eternity. Their soul's salvation depended on their telling the truth. The Bible tells us that liars will be cast into hell. They would have been awful hypocrites to profess faith in Jesus and then tell the public a big lie.
>
> When we read their writings and see how they gave their lives in martyrdom, we know that they were not liars. Men of such caliber do not lie. Jesus Christ, who knew all things, had made the statement that His "Words

shall not pass away" (Matt. 24:35). We can be assured
that we have a truthful account of the Gospel in the Bible.

As DeShazer eagerly read the Bible particularly the
promises in the Bible, he was more and more brought to
the point where he felt the message of the Gospel was for
him as an individual. He came to believe that "all of
these things were written and all of these events took
place so that I can know that I have eternal life if I believe on Jesus Christ."

Increasingly the desire grew in his heart to know that
he himself had been pardoned from his sins and that he
might know the joy of forgiveness. He realized that he
was a sinner. He came to realize afresh that God hates
sin. He read in the Gospel where Jesus said, "Repent
ye, and believe the gospel" (Mark 1:15). The Heavenly
Father did not mock this spiritually starved lonely American boy. The light finally broke, and DeShazer knew—
that salvation was his.

CHAPTER IX

REMARKABLE CONVERSION

For days DeShazer, more or less unwittingly, had been moving toward the crisis point. The prayers of his parents certainly had followed him. The prayers of former friends had ascended to the throne of God in his behalf. The Word of God through the precious Book had been illuminated by the Holy Spirit, and certainly the presence of Christ speaking to his inner consciousness and knocking at his heart's door had made an impression. But all of these factors would have been of no avail without DeShazer's meeting the conditions. This he did. The miracle of conversion took place June 8, 1944.

DeShazer had been reading Rom. 10:9, "If thou shalt confess with thy mouth the Lord Jesus and shalt believe in thine heart that God hath raised him from the dead, thou shalt be saved." He had read that passage many times, but on this particular day, somehow it became a power in his own life. He laid hold upon it as the very Word of God. In prayer he said: "Lord, you know all things. You know I do repent of my sins. Even though I am far from home and though I am in prison, I must have forgiveness."

As he meditated and prayed along this line, there came into his soul a divine joy, a soul rest, an inner witness that God for Christ's sake had forgiven him.

There was not much he could do with respect to changing his way of living. There came over him a sense that God wanted obedience. He was just simple enough to tell the Lord that he would obey. He yielded his spirit, his plans, his hopes, his aspirations. It was then he learned the truth which he has mentioned over and over since that time. "Obedience to God is the way to eternal life." In writing about his glorious experience on that happy day he says:

> My heart was filled with joy. I wouldn't have traded places with anyone at that time. Oh, what a great joy it was to know that I was saved, that God had forgiven me of my sins and that I had become "partaker of the divine nature" (II Pet. 1:4). Though I was unworthy and sinful, I had "redemption through his blood, the forgiveness of sins, according to the riches of his grace" (Eph. 1:7).
>
> Hunger, starvation, and a freezing cold prison cell no longer had horrors for me. They would be only for a passing moment. Even death could hold no threat when I knew that God had saved me. Death is just one more trial that I must go through before I can enjoy the pleasures of eternal life. There will be no pain, no suffering, no sorrow, no loneliness in heaven. Everything will be perfect with joy forever. I had the promise of being like Jesus who is God's Son. In that day I will know all things, for I will then be a partaker of immortality.

The time when DeShazer would have to give up the copy of the Bible was drawing near. He memorized as much of the Scriptures as possible. He would go over and over certain portions and re-memorize so as to keep them fresh in his mind. One is amazed at his ability under the circumstances to memorize so much and to have it for ready reference during the remaining fourteen months he was in prison.

Becoming a Christian, however, did not change the outward environment of DeShazer's life. He was still in prison. Perhaps he would never get out. He had the same guards, the same obligation to remain in solitary confinement, the same intolerable food, and the absence of fellowship.

But DeShazer had made his decision. He had believed on the Lord Jesus Christ. He had become a Christian. Now as a Christian he was going to do his best to live the way a Christian should.

He knew he had been weak in self-control and in will power. In his early life he had been taught to love people and to be friendly to all. Seldom had he permitted himself to do this. In his reading of the Bible, he found much emphasis upon loving one another. He knew in other days he had been disobedient to his parents and that throughout the years he had been disobedient to God and to his own conscience. All of this was sin. But now through the grace of the Lord Jesus Christ he was forgiven for all those wrongs.

What he wanted now was divine strength. He wanted to strengthen his self-control and gain a new grip on his will power. Many lessons were necessary for him to learn to trust the Lord. In John 1:12 he read, "As many as received him to them gave he power to become the sons of God." It was that power which he needed and which he wanted.

He remembered the attitudes and feelings he had had before his conversion. He remembered that just before his change of heart he had become very angry. One day during the period he was supposed to be cleaning his cell, one of the guards came along and yelled at him, "Hurry up." This made DeShazer angry, and almost before he knew it, he told the guard in English, "Go, jump in the lake." Naturally the guard didn't like this. DeShazer describes the incident:

Before I knew what was going to happen, the door was unlocked, and the guard hit me on the head with his fist. I immediately kicked him in the stomach with my bare foot, and he hit me with his steel scabbard. I had been using some water on the floor to mop up my cell. I picked up the dirty mop water and threw it on the guard. It cooled him off enough so that he didn't do any more than swear at me. But it is strange that he didn't cut off my head. This was not the way that I had been taught to make friends.

But that was before DeShazer accepted the way of Christ. After he became a Christian, his attitude changed. He knew it, and in due time his guards knew it and so did his comrades. In John 13:34 Jesus said, "Love one another." This is a commandment of God. Again DeShazer was seized with the meaning of obedience. He says:

God expects us to keep His commandments. The only way we know we are saved is to keep the commandments of Christ. I found out when I read the Bible that it was necessary to be obedient. God hates sin and disobedience. We cannot please God if we continue doing those things that we know are wrong. If we accept Jesus and continue in sin, we will be like the seed in the parable which fell on stony ground and when it sprung up because it had no depth of soil soon withered and died. (Matt. 13:3-9.)

When Jesus was on earth, he warned people not to be led astray by the human desire to do their own will. In Matt. 7:21, Jesus said, "Not every one that saith unto me, Lord, Lord, shall enter into the kingdom of heaven; but he that doeth the will of my Father which is in heaven." Obedience is what God has required from the beginning of the history of mankind. If we accept Jesus, we must be obedient or be cast out of the kingdom of God.

When I memorized I John 2:3-6, I found it was necessary to be obedient. I wanted to know that I was a real Christian and not a hypocrite. These verses tell us we can know: "And hereby we do know that we know him if we keep his commandments. He that saith, I know him, and keepeth not his commandments, is a liar, and the truth is not in him. But whoso keepeth his word, in him verily is the love of God perfected: hereby know we that we are in him. He that saith he abideth in him ought himself also so to walk, even as he walked."

Submission to Jesus brings a wonderful peace. I came to realize that my life would be more enjoyable if I were obedient. I found at first it was hard to do what I knew was right. I had much trouble for more than three weeks. The habits of swearing, vulgar thoughts, and telling lies did not immediately leave me when I accepted Jesus. However, when these manifestations of sin appeared I asked for forgiveness right away. The promise of I John 1:9 says, "If we confess our sins, he is faithful and just to forgive us our sins, and to cleanse us from all un-righteousness." God always keeps His promises and since I did my part all unrighteousness was taken away.

Since DeShazer felt the command of God was to love his fellow men, and since the only individuals he was privileged to meet were guards, he was waiting for an opportunity to demonstrate his love to them. An opportunity thus to test his new-found love and his determination to love others soon came. One day as he was being taken back to his cell by one of the guards, something happened which brought this matter very forcibly to his mind. For some reason the guard was in a special hurry. While they were on their way toward the cell, the guard slapped DeShazer on the back with his hand and ordered, "Hiaku, hiaku!" (Hurry up! hurry up!) When they came to the door of the cell, he opened the door a little and shoved DeShazer inside. Unfortunately, before DeShazer could get through the door, the guard slammed it and caught DeShazer's foot. Instead of opening the door to release his foot, the guard began kicking De-

Shazer's bare foot with his hobnailed boots. Finally,
DeShazer was able to push the door open and get his
foot free. He jumped inside. In recalling this incident,
DeShazer admits that he felt resentment and hatred for
the guard. At the same time, an inner voice told him
that he should love the guard. Matthew 5:44 came to
mind in which Jesus said, "Love your enemies, bless
them that curse you, do good to them that hate you,
and pray for them which despitefully use you, and persecute you."

Such an experience would be a real test to most new
converts. In referring to his thinking in this connection
DeShazer says:

> Jesus' words were coming to my mind, but at first I
> wished that I couldn't remember them. There was no
> way, however, by which I could get out of this predica-
> ment. I had promised obedience if God showed me the
> way. God had helped me to memorize the Sermon on
> the Mount so that He could use it to show me the way at
> this particular time. God was being faithful to show me
> the way. The only thing I could do was to submit and be
> obedient. Any other course would have meant God's dis-
> pleasure, but by obedience God is pleased.

Other Scripture also came flooding DeShazer's mind
"Submit yourselves, therefore, to God. Resist the devil
and he will flee from you. Draw nigh to God, and he
will draw nigh to you. Cleanse your hands, ye sinners
and purify your hearts, ye double minded. Be afflicted
and mourn, and weep: let your laughter be turned to
mourning, and your joy to heaviness. Humble yourselve
in the sight of the Lord, and he shall lift you up" (Ja
4:7-10).

Then, too, the thirteenth chapter of I Corinthians—
the great love chapter—came to his mind. Since being

freed from prison, this is one of DeShazer's favorite Scriptures. As a matter of fact he quotes it perhaps more than any other portion of the Bible using, as a rule, James Moffatt's translation: "Love is very patient, very kind. Love knows no jealousy; love makes no parade, gives itself no airs, is never rude, never selfish, never irritated, never resentful; love is never glad when others go wrong, love is gladdened by goodness, always slow to expose, always eager to believe the best, always hopeful, always patient. Love never disappears."

Herein lies the depth of DeShazer's consecration to return to Japan. The Gospel truly meant to him, "Love your enemies." The way DeShazer puts this in his own words is most interesting:

> I had seen people who could show a beautiful attitude in very trying circumstances, but I did not know that we can all have the kind of love that is long-suffering, kind, and patient. However, if we are given the commandment to love one another, it is surely possible for us actually to do so. Since God has given the commandment to love, our part of the transaction is to put forth an effort and try to have love for others. This would be a wonderful world if we would all try to love one another. If we would honestly try and if we would recognize Jesus as God's Son and our Saviour, God would be pleased with us. I made up my mind to try.

So it was that the very next morning after he had felt resentment and hatred for the guard who had kicked his foot, he had a chance to try to love some one, and in this instance, to love an enemy. As the guard came on duty, DeShazer moved toward the door of his cell and said, "Ohayoo gozaimasu." (Good morning.) Imagine the surprise of the guard. He looked in the direction of DeShazer with a puzzled expression. Perhaps he thought the prisoner had gone stark crazy. The guard, however, made no significant comment. Several mornings went by with DeShazer trying to be friendly.

One morning as the guard came on duty, he walked immediately over to DeShazer's cell and spoke to him through the door. He was smiling. DeShazer, at that time, knew but little Japanese, but he was able to talk to the guard enough to ask him how many brothers and sisters he had. This seemed to please the guard.

On another morning soon after this, he saw the guard walking up and down the corridor of the prison with his hands in a prayerful attitude and his lips moving. After a while the guard came over to DeShazer's cell and started to speak to him. He told him that he had been praying to his mother who had died when he was a small boy. This was in harmony with the guard's belief.

This particular guard became very friendly to De-Shazer and from that time on did not shout at him nor treat him rudely. On one occasion, the guard slid back the little door and handed DeShazer a boiled sweet potato. This was a wonderful treat. DeShazer says he was already getting some of the pay-off for being gracious to his enemies. At another time the guard gave him five figs and some candy. Again DeShazer was convinced that God's way is the best way. Moralizing on this he says:

> How easy it was to make a friend out of an enemy because I had just tried. God's way will work if we will try it out. Jesus was not an idealist whose ideals could not be realized. When He told us to love one another, He told us the best way to act, and it *will work*. His way will work out better than any other way which could be tried, but people and nations still try some other way to their own confusion.

It was easy to tell that my nature had been changed. I had a different attitude toward life. It had all come about through the promises in the Bible. When we see those promises and know that they are true, our nature will be changed if we submit to God's will and accept Jesus. I had met the conditions in the promises, and I knew that God would do His part. God has promised to come and dwell in our hearts. I John 4: 15 says, "Whosoever shall confess that Jesus is the Son of God, God dwelleth in him, and he in God." I had confessed that Jesus is the Son of God, and God was dwelling in my heart.

There was new power in my life. I had been weak in self-control and will power, but now I had power so that I could even love my enemies. It all came from heaven. I knew that it was supernatural. Jesus had gone to heaven, and He is existing in the form of God in heaven now. His spirit comes right into our hearts when we are obedient to Him and confess that He is the Son of God. We make friends with God and God loves us and delights in us. The Bible says in John 1: 12, "As many as received him, to them gave he power to become the sons of God, even to them that believe on his name." It is God that gives the power after we meet certain specified conditions. With the Spirit of Jesus dwelling in our hearts we are able to love our fellow men. The world needs Jesus. We need to recognize God's Son. Without Jesus Christ we have hatred and terrible wars.

We all know that wars lead to hardship and heartache. We hate war, but we still continue to fight. As individuals we often have the same trouble, for we know what is the right thing to do, but we lack the will power or the self-control to go ahead and do what we know is right. I observed this when I was on the airplane leaving Japan at the time of the bombing. Long before that time I had made up my mind not to shoot at civilians, but in spite of my resolutions I had shot at civilians. It is wrong to do things that are harmful to the body. It is wrong to be resentful and provoked with others. I had often wished that I could live a life which was free from doing those things that I knew were wrong. But sin had brought constant defeat in my life throughout the years.

It was a great joy to me to find Jesus and to learn that He gives power to overcome such a defeated life. Herein lies the difference between a Christian and a person who is not a Christian. A Christian is "cleansed from all unrighteousness." A Christian lives a victorious life. The power which Jesus gives keeps us from doing what we know is wrong. Jesus gives self-control and will power to all people who are weak on these points. By living such a victorious life we have the witness that we know Jesus.

CHAPTER X

HOTTEST SUMMER AND COLDEST WINTER IN PRISON

Twenty-six months of grueling experience in a Japanese war prison had weakened the health of DeShazer and his three comrades. The fact that DeShazer had accepted Christ had given him inner spiritual fortitude, but it had not rebuilt his physical life. The summer of 1944 was extremely hot at Nanking. In the intense heat, the prison cells in the low wood frame buildings were almost unbearable in the daytime. Even at night it was so sultry it was difficult to rest. Along with the weather conditions was the inhumane manner of the prison construction. The doors of the prison cells were made of solid wood. There was no way to ventilate the cells, no circulation of air.

Lieutenant Hite became very ill with an extremely high fever. When it became apparent that his very life was in jeopardy, the Japanese guards began to give him some attention. Apparently, they had been reprimanded for their carelessness in connection with the death of Lieutenant Meder. They removed the solid wood door from Lieutenant Hite's cell and replaced it with a screen door. This made it possible for a passage of air through the little high window down through the door. In spite of this, Hite's fever continued dangerously high.

Much to the relief of Hite's comrades and, of course, to himself the Japanese officials began to take serious interest in his welfare and made an unusual effort to bring him back to health. A medical assistant was given the duty of looking after him. Apparently he was told to spare no effort to save him. DeShazer reports that often he could hear the Japanese bringing ice to put on Hite's feverish head. The young physician actually moved into the prison himself so that he could be near Hite in order to take care of him. Under the patient care of this young medical assistant and with the advent of cooler weather, Hite began to mend.

Throughout the unbearable days and nights during the summer of 1944, DeShazer himself tired and weary, was receiving unusual encouragement and strength because of his new-found love. Within himself he had the witness of the presence of the Lord. Days, weeks, and months had now passed since he had had the privilege of reading the Bible. But the Scripture that he had memorized was becoming well known to him. The first Epistle of John was one of his favorites. He had memorized all five chapters and made special use of the teachings concerning abiding in the Lord. Again and again there recurred to his mind the importance of the commandments of God and the necessity of being *obedient*. Such Scriptures were recalled as; "Hereby we do know that we know him, if we keep his commandments." DeShazer says concerning this truth, "I knew that I knew Him because I was able by the power He gives actually to keep His commandments."

Almost in a soliloquy he would become subjective and talk to himself somewhat along this line:

That's a good method to tell whether anyone is a Christian. Anyone who keeps God's commandments is a Christian. I have faith that the blood of Jesus covers all of my sins. I know that Jesus died for me, consequently

I can ask myself the question, "Am I doing what I think is right to the best of my ability or am I doing anything that I know is wrong, willfully?" If I am not willfully disobedient and I am trying to do what I know to be right, I am living up to all the light that God has given me. I am keeping His commandments and the Bible says that I know Him if I keep His commandments.

During the long, hot summer, the hours of the day dragged slowly. The prisoners could look out the little window and see the blue sky. How they longed to get outside and fix their eyes on something besides the four walls of their cells. The few precious moments they were allowed outside each day were a great relief, but, oh, how quickly they passed!

One of the most interesting observations of DeShazer throughout his entire prison experience took place in the summer of 1944. The entire heavens became a calendar to him. He had noticed, as he looked out the little window at night, in the summer of 1943, the different star formations. He knew some of them and observed how they gradually disappeared from the range of his vision as they moved from the zenith to the south. In particular, he had noticed the constellation Scorpio. Finally, it disappeared out of range. Now as the summer of 1944 came, this constellation once more began to rise to where he could see it through the window. When it finally came to the same position that he had remembered in 1943, he knew a full year had passed. Once again, as he observed the handiwork of God, he was made to thank the Lord for His dealings with him. He says:

It was hard to realize the fact that the One who formed the whole creation would be concerned over a small creature like me. However, I knew from God's Word

that this is true, and God's spirit agrees with His Word.
The Spirit of God must bear witness to us before we can
know that we are saved.

Fall came with more moderate temperatures. Weeks
passed, and finally the beginning of a very bad winter,
the winter of 1944-45. There was a heavy snow fall the
first of December. From that time on there was snow in
the prison yard until the first of March. It was the coldest winter the men experienced throughout their entire
imprisonment.

The guards brought heavier clothes, and, as the winter
became more severe, they finally returned to the men their
old army clothes. These were put on over the Japanese
garments. To the credit of the Japanese prison at Nanking it must be said that the men were able to keep their
clothes much cleaner than in the prison at Shanghai.
This was a new prison, and fortunately there were no
lice. In the former prison they were constantly plagued
by the presence of lice. The only redeeming feature in
connection with the lice was that it did occupy their time
to quite an extent in hunting them out from their clothes
and crushing them between their thumbnails.

It was two or three weeks after the first heavy snow-
fall before the guards took the men out into the prison
yard for exercise. At this time the prisoners cleaned
their cells. After they had finished, they were told to carry
out some exercise but were warned not to take off their
slippers. The slippers which they had, however, were
of the loose Japanese kind, and it was impossible for them
to run without losing them. With snow on the ground it
was impossible to exercise without jumping and running.
They walked around the yard two or three times but
were eager to run in order to get warmed up. (This was

the only time of the day that they were able to get warm.)
They finally ignored the order, kicked off their slippers,
and started running barefooted.

There was a penalty to pay! As soon as the guards
saw them running without their slippers, they ordered
them to stop and go back into their cells. Naturally their
feet were dirty since in some of the places where they
had been running the snow had melted and the ground
was muddy. The men started for the building expecting to go inside to wash their feet at the water hydrant.
The guards, however, rushed them away and told them to
go over to the snowbank and clean their feet in the snow.

The men told the guards that they would rather wash
their feet at the water hydrant. Still the guards insisted
that they go to the snowbank. Lieutenant Barr resenting
their orders tried to go inside. One of the guards
grabbed him and tried to turn him around by taking hold
of his coat sleeve. Barr, however, with considerable
energy jabbed his elbow into the guard's stomach. This
made the guards even more angry and Lieutenant Barr
was kept outside after his comrades were taken to their
cells.

Then Lieutenant Barr paid dearly for his deed. It
seems that about ten guards began beating him. To their
surprise Lieutenant Barr, six feet two inches tall, was
more alert and stronger than they expected. Not disposed
to submit willingly to a whipping, Barr gave the guards
a rather rough time. Finally, they were able to shove
him along and put him into his cell. Then it was that the
captain of the prison was called to help give discipline.
Barr was placed in a strait jacket, his arms were tied
behind his back, and ropes were drawn so tight that his
shoulder nearly broke. His chest, too, was being sub-

jected to such awful tension by the ropes around his body that the pain was excruciating. To the other men it "sounded as if Barr was being killed from where they were in the prison cells. He was certainly doing a good job of hollering."

The screaming was undoubtedly due to the physical torture, but it also had a wholesome, psychological effect on the prison official who, according to DeShazer, "was really a kind-hearted, tender-spirited man." One of the guards, Mr. Misaka, who had tried to be a gentleman and a good friend made an effort to persuade the others to release Barr. This they did after about one hour of torture. The guards seemed to feel rather virtuous for they told Lieutenant Barr that he was fortunate because they tortured their own men by that means from four to six hours when they had occasion to discipline them.

The whole experience in connection with the Barr incident once again brought dejection of spirit among the prisoners. They wondered if there never would be an end to prison life and the recurrence of such experiences. Fortunately, it was only a short time before their hopes were again lifted. This time it was more than better food or a kindly guard. The most welcome news they had had in many, many months came on Christmas Day, 1944. It seems impossible that the appearance of bombers could be a welcome sound and sight, but such it was for these American flyers when for the first time they realized that American dive bombers had reached Nanking. The elation of the prisoners was almost unbounded. They could actually see the dive bombers skimming over the house tops. They were shooting as they came. They could hear the Japanese shooting back at them apparently with every weapon that they could procure. Soon they could hear bombs exploding and could see great clouds of black smoke billowing toward the sky. Evidently some oil refineries and storage tanks had been the targets.

The satisfaction which came to the minds of the prisoners when they knew that Americans were deep in China was inexpressible. For many months the Japanese guards had been telling them extreme stories regarding the losses of the United States and the successes of the Japanese. Repeatedly they would say that the Japanese had taken possession of San Francisco and New York, that Japanese soldiers were marching up and down the streets of these and other cities giving orders to the American people. Secretly, of course, the American airmen had been looking day after day for the appearance of American airplanes. Month after month had come and gone without any such appearance. Sometimes they had wondered if the stories being told by the Japanese guards were true.

Evidently the Japanese officials believed the stories they were telling, for they were apparently taken completely by surprise by the appearance of the American planes. They were able, quickly, to adjust to the situation, for they were soon telling the Americans that the United States planes had dropped a few bombs in the rivers and had killed a few fish. The thought of Japan ever having to surrender seemed completely foreign to their thinking. The American planes, however, brought no relief to the intense cold inside the Japanese prison. The long, cold winter continued. DeShazer and his comrades were constantly suffering with colds. Finally DeShazer began breaking out with large boils. Sometimes boils would appear on the bottoms of his feet. These continued through the remainder of the winter. When warmer weather came, the boils disappeared for a time but unfortunately reappeared later in the summer.

For some reason not known to the American airmen they were made ready for another long overland trip. It was the middle of June when one morning they were taken out of their cells, once again handcuffed and tied up in preparation for the move. It must have been interesting to see the guards shake hands with the men in this handcuffed position. Despite the fact that one group was guards and the other was prisoners there had been built up a real sense of friendship. They had been together in the Nanking prison from April, 1943, to the middle of June 1945—more than twenty-six months. This was a full year after DeShazer's conversion.

They rode by train in a northerly direction for more than forty hours. At that time they did not know where they were going. Everywhere they went, they realized they were traveling through strange country and seeing strange appearing crowds. Their hands and legs were tied with their belts. Each man had a guard who hung on to the rope whether they were sitting or standing. Over each man was a large green raincoat. Over each head was pulled a hat which had a mask for a face.

The train was crowded beyond all description. Most of the passengers were soldiers. Some, however, were civilians and some were Red Cross workers. All of the women, of course, were out in the aisles sitting on the floor or on some of the baggage. The men in the Japanese program are the ones who occupy the seats. High ranking officers would come into the car and order someone of lower rank to get up and give him a place. Sometimes Chinese men or women would try to get through the car, but someone would order them out, and, if they

didn't understand, a slap of the hand would convince
them that they were to stay out. The whole group, however, seemed to be a serious, tired-looking crowd of
people.

Everyone was surprised to see the prisoners wearing
the peculiar masks, but no one dared to ask questions.
DeShazer describes one incident which seemed to him
amusing:

> A Japanese mother brought her two children up rather
> close to our masked faces. While the children with sur-
> prised faces were looking at us, the mother for sheer fun
> silently moved away. As the children looked at us and
> our peculiar masks, they screamed out in fright. This
> caused everyone in the train to laugh, and the mother re-
> turned smiling to comfort her children.

In this grotesque situation, however, DeShazer was
not unmindful of his dedication to God. He says:

> While riding on the train, I remembered the Bible mes-
> sage. I wondered what God was going to do with all of
> these souls as these people didn't know Jesus. They had
> probably never heard of Him. I thanked God for his
> mercy to me in allowing me the privilege of reading the
> Bible. I was glad for a Christian home and my parents'
> prayers which God had heard. I wished there was some
> way the people on the train could know about the salva-
> tion which God had provided for all people. What joy
> they would know if Jesus were dwelling in their hearts as
> he was dwelling in mine!

After nearly three days of thus journeying in a strange
country, shackled down and with hoods over their faces,
they arrived in Peking. Just before coming into the
station, the guards told the prisoners where they were. It
was an extremely hot day, and, after leaving the train, the
prisoners were taken to the side of the station to wait in

a shady place for a military truck. People seemed to be everywhere. Many Chinese were lying in the shade of the railroad station. As the guards with their prisoners came near, these loafers were told to clear out and make way.

One old Chinese lady who had a great deal of baggage was unable to get out of the way rapidly enough. One of the Japanese officers started screaming at the woman to hurry. Obviously, the poor woman was hurrying as fast as her age would allow. This, however, was not sufficient. The officer went over and slapped her on both sides of the face in an effort to make her really hurry. This treatment seemed to be common almost everywhere. DeShazer says, "It made me wish that they could be shown the way of love."

Finally, a truck came and took the guards and prisoners to a large prison in Peking. Apparently it was a military prison with more than one thousand Japanese prisoners receiving typical Oriental punishment for some misconduct. Five or six of the Japanese soldier prisoners were placed in a prison cell together and for two hours were forced to kneel on the floor without changing position. After such a two-hour period they were all supposed to sit on the floor, straight up, feet out in front, without any support for their backs.

The situation around Peking was decidedly different from what the Americans had experienced around Nanking. The guards at Nanking were constantly talking about the Japanese people having a higher standard of living than the Chinese. They were frequently claiming that Japan was the leading nation in the world for cleanliness and decency. After having traveled some six hundred miles deeper into China, DeShazer admits that he could easily see why the Japanese felt their manner of living was better than the Chinese. At the same time the American airmen were trying to tell their guards how much better things were in America. DeShazer says:

> We tried to tell them about the food and the automobiles, but it seemed like a fairy tale to them. They thought America was a place where bandits flourished and waxed rich. Soldiers in the Japanese Army are accustomed to being slapped by an officer of higher rank. When we told them there was no slapping in the U. S. Army, they said that was impossible, for they thought there would be no discipline.

The American prisoners now were no longer to have the joy even of a prison courtyard. The poor, persecuted Chinese might be everywhere through the city of Peking, but the quartet of American prisoners were placed in the inner section of this Japanese military prison. Each one was placed in a solitary cell, and from that time on there was no more going outside for exercise. The only time they were to see each other at all was when they were allowed to get together for a bath, once a week.

Very frequently the Americans could hear and occasionally see the guards take the soldiers out of their cells and beat them. This apparently was one of their chief methods of keeping discipline. It was difficult for De-Shazer to think he was in a real world. There was so much cruelty and fear. He was constantly reminded that freedom is one of the great heritages in the United States not known in a non-Christian country.

CHAPTER XI

NEAR DEATH—
ANOTHER UNUSUAL SPIRITUAL EXPERIENCE

When the American prisoners were first put into solitary confinement in the Peking Japanese prison, they were forced to sit on the floor just as the other prisoners were. The American men, however, were not accustomed to sitting on the floor. The whole experience became so excruciating that the guards were finally persuaded to provide some relief. Relief it was to the men under the circumstances, but, when we think of the arrangement in ordinary life, it seems unbearable.

Sometimes DeShazer refers to the relief that was provided in terms of a "bench." A small bench, he says, was provided for each of the American men to sit on. The facts are, it was far from a bench, for it was essentially a little stool with a top made of a two by four, about eight inches long. Throughout the entire day each man was required to sit on this most uncomfortable seat. He was not allowed to move around in the cell at all. The men were told to sit three feet from the wall and keep their faces toward the rear wall. Evidently, the Japanese did not want the Americans to see some of the brutal treatment which their own soldiers received.

Many people even in normal health, subjected to this kind of treatment, would undoubtedly crack up mentally in a short time. It is difficult to imagine the mental torment experienced by these men who had gone through thirty-eight months of deprivation, hunger, sickness, and punishment. With DeShazer, one month was all he could stand. Already his body was weakened by severe attacks of dysentery; he was much emaciated. Boils appeared again—this time all over his body. He reports that he counted as many as seventy-five bad boils at one time. Of course, he was no longer able to sit on the little stool. He lay on his bed mat day after day.

After about three weeks of this he became somewhat delirious. He was a very sick man; he describes his condition as follows:

> I still kept going over the verses in the Bible that I had memorized. I thought it wouldn't be long before I would be in heaven with Lieutenant Meder. My heart was hurting and I could remember how Lieutenant Meder said his heart had hurt before he died. Several of the Nanking guards had told me that the reason Meder died was that his heart had stopped. I thought I would probably die for the same reason.

Experiences of this kind went on for several days. Finally, Matt. 17:20 came to mind. "If ye have faith as a grain of mustard seed, ye shall say unto this mountain, Remove hence to yonder place; and it shall remove; and nothing shall be impossible unto you." He began to think about how small a mustard seed is and then he thought, "Surely I have that much faith—that God can make me well!"

Apparently, the Holy Spirit was leading him into a new experience. His comment regarding what he went through is most gripping. Many, undoubtedly, would not understand it. Without doubt, the blessed Holy Spirit understanding his weakened condition came and like the ministering angels with Christ himself, in Gethsemane, ministered unto him:

Many times I had thanked God for faith to believe that I was saved. When I had just believed, then God had shown me that I was saved. It now seemed to me that God wished for me to have faith that He would heal me from my bad attack of dysentery. God had been such a good friend to me that I felt I could not act as a coward now. The only thing to do was to try it out and see if God was really talking to me.

I got out of bed and sat on the little bench one morning after I had prayed it all out with God. I was so weak that my heart could have stopped very easy, but God knows how to keep a person's heart going. I didn't know what to expect. I just prayed that God would make me better. I made up my mind to sit there until I either passed out or God healed me.

It was not long before the voice of God broke into my thoughts. This was different from anything I had experienced before. I had often wondered where a person's thoughts come from and as I sat in prison I used to be conscious of the activity of my thoughts. Ordinarily, I had control over them, but now it was different. I still had control over my thoughts, yet I knew that I was being possessed by another power. I was sure I was not responsible for the thoughts coming to my mind. I had never dreamed of anything like this. It was hard for me to realize that I was experiencing such a glorious contact with God.

"It is the Holy Spirit who is speaking to you," the mysterious voice said, "The Holy Spirit has made you free." I immediately began to wonder if I was going to get out of prison. The voice said, "You are free to do as you please. You can go through the wall or jump over the wall. You are free." I couldn't figure that out, but I never made any attempt to jump over the wall. I knew that I was free, but I had only a desire to do what was pleasing to God. "The Holy Spirit has set you free from sin," I was told.

Free from sin! Yes, God's Word has said, "Whosoever abideth in him, sinneth not: whosoever sinneth hath not seen him, neither known him." This was in the first

Epistle of John that I had memorized. It was the third chapter and sixth verse. I was free from any desire to do willful sin. If I knew something was wrong, I would put forth every effort I could not to do it any more. James 4:17 states, "Therefore to him that knoweth to do good, and doeth it not, to him it is sin." This is the kind of sin that God expects us to live above today. The sin of ignorance spoken of in Leviticus is all taken care of by the blood of Jesus. We have been given power by Jesus to be free from willful, disobedient sin.

I was able to tell by this reasoning that the voice speaking to me agreed with the Bible. The Spirit and the Word agree. I was almost too happy for this world. I had been lonesome and sick, but now God spoke to me and filled my heart with an unearthly joy.

I found out that I could ask questions and I could receive answers right away. This was a big help to me in connection with my food. I was always hungry, but, often, if I ate the food, I would become very sick. When the food came to the door, I would pray and ask if I should eat the food or should I send it back. If the voice said, "Yes, yes," I would eat; but if the answer was, "No, no," I would send the food back. For two days I was not given permission to eat or to drink. I was weak but the sickness was leaving me.

I would not lie down in the daytime if I was not sure that it was permissible for me to do so. My body was tired and weak, but I wanted to be sure and show "faith as a grain of mustard seed." As I was sitting on the little seat facing the wall, I wondered if there wasn't some way that I could let the guards know about the wonderful spirit of Jesus which was so present with me. His power and life were throbbing with a thrilling consciousness to me at every heart beat.

There didn't seem to be much that I could do, but I remembered the story about Daniel. I went down on my knees in front of the door, folded my hands to pray, and I really did pray. The first guard came by, beat on the door with his sword and hollered at me to get back on my bench. It was against the rules for any prisoner even

to look at the door. Japanese prisoners received a beating
for such audacity, but I did not move when the guard
shouted. I felt no fear since God had shown me what to
do. I felt a great weight of joy.

In a very short time the guard returned with several
other guards. The door opened and the guards walked
into my cell. They never hit me nor hollered at me. They
acted a little awed. A medical man came to the cell, and
I was picked up and laid down on a straw mat. The
medical man rolled up my shirt sleeve and shot some
medicine into my arm after which I was left alone in my
cell to thank Jesus who was close by my side.

When meal time came, I was surprised to receive a nice
pint of milk, boiled eggs, some good well-made bread and
some nice, nourishing soup. I couldn't help crying and
laughing when I thought how beautifully and wonderfully
God had worked this all out for me. From that time
until we were released from prison I received milk, eggs,
bread, and good nourishing food. I stayed in bed because
I thought that God had indicated that this was the thing
for me to do.

The foregoing experience was wonderful in every way
to DeShazer. Next to his wonderful experience of conversion some fourteen months before, this was the most
wonderful spiritual experience he had ever enjoyed.

On August 10, 1945, he had another type of experience
which will always remain sacred to him. He says that on
this notable day when he first woke up in the morning
he was told to "start praying."

I asked, "What shall I pray about?" Pray for peace,
and pray without ceasing, I was told. I had prayed
about peace but very little, if at all before that time, as
it seemed useless. I thought God could stop the war any
time with the power which he had manifested.

But God was now teaching me the lesson of cooperation.
It was God's joy for me to be willing to let Him use me.
God does use human instruments to accomplish His will

Starvation and Torture—Then Freedom and Smiles
This picture was taken soon after DeShazer was released from prison at the
close of the war by American paratroopers.

Lt. Robt. T. Hite **Captain C. J. Nielson**

Two of DeShazer's comrades in prison. The three with Lt. George Barr were
set free Aug. 20, 1945.

On Homeward Flight

DeShazer, Nielson, Hite and others stop en route to U. S. from North China via India.

here on earth. It will be a great joy to us through all eternity if we can cooperate with Him. I started to pray for peace although I had a very poor idea of what was taking place in the world at that time.

About seven o'clock in the morning I began to pray. It seemed very easy to pray on the subject of peace. I prayed that God would put a great desire in the hearts of the Japanese leaders for peace. I thought about the days of peace that would follow. Japanese people would no doubt be discouraged, and I felt sympathetic toward them. I prayed that God would not allow them to fall into persecution by the victorious armies.

At two o'clock in the afternoon the Holy Spirit told me, "You don't need to pray any more. The victory is won." I was amazed. I thought that this was quicker and better than the regular method of receiving world news. Probably this news broadcast had not come over the radio to America as yet. I thought I would just wait and see what was to happen.

DeShazer, of course, had no radio. He was not privileged for several days to get the news of that fateful tenth day of August, 1945. We now know that that was the day when the first atomic bomb was dropped on Hiroshima. It was then that the Japanese leaders began to sue for peace. He learned about this later, and once again he was convinced that God had been teaching him a lesson in cooperation. From that day forward he began to put great stress upon the fact that God wants us to pray, that God hears and answers prayer, that God knows the best way.

The next ten days and nights constitute a most interesting period in DeShazer's life of continuous joy. He says:

I felt the love of God flooding my soul. Night and day a rapturous joy was being experienced. I felt certain that I was having a foretaste of heaven.

At the same time new strength was coming to his weakened body. He was now receiving plenty of good food. Vitality was returning. It was almost sheer ecstasy as he lay on his straw mat to realize both the wonder of returning physical strength and at the same time to experience the joy of the fullness of the Holy Spirit.

> I promised God that I would make restitution for the things that I had stolen. I felt certain that I would be able to return to the United States. I was going to make amends as far as God showed me it was the right thing to do. It was a wonderful feeling not to harbor any resentment or ill will toward any one. I felt love toward the Japanese people and a deep interest in their welfare. I felt that we were all made by the same God and that we must share our hardships and our happiness together. How I wished that I could tell the Japanese people about Jesus! I knew that my Saviour would be their Saviour, too. I realized that Jesus died for our sins, that he was alive today and that although He died so that He might become our Saviour, He is coming back again to reign as our King for ever and ever. Jesus was as real and alive to me as anyone could possibly be.

He had had news from heaven that the victory had been won. As yet, however, no word had been received from any guard concerning developments. One day, as he looked out the window, he saw smoke and burnt paper rising up in the sky. As the guards came on duty, he observed they were wearing new clothes. He saw them discarding old clothes and breaking into their supplies. He felt within himself that these were the first signs that the end had come.

His heart was beating faster and faster as he thought about the freedom that would soon be his. Then it was that his thoughts were directed to the Japanese.

I could not help wondering what would happen to Japan now. Their hopes had been set on victory. It would be an awful blow to suffer defeat. But, if the Japanese found out about Jesus, the military defeat to them would in reality be a great victory. At this time the voice of the Holy Spirit spoke to me clearly, "You are called to go and teach the Japanese people and to go wherever I send you."

It seemed difficult for him to believe that God would call him to such an important work. He knew he had never had any ability as a public speaker. He knew he had lacked training and Bible study. He recalled that he had always seemed to be "as dry as a rock," when he wanted to tell something. At the same time he realized that he had promised God that he would do God's will. Once more in his inner soul he agreed that he would co-operate with the Lord.

I thought perhaps I could be a janitor in some church, but God's voice was telling me to "get in and work for all you are worth. You have as good a chance as anyone else." I knew that I could try, and I had already been shown the power of Jesus, if we have "faith as a grain of mustard seed."

CHAPTER XII

END OF WAR—
FREEDOM AT LAST—WELCOME HOME

On August 20, 1945, just ten days after his wonderful experience of praying for peace, freedom came to DeShazer and his comrades. Forty months of imprisonment and punishment abruptly came to an end! A Japanese official announced, "The war is over. You can go home now." Those were wonderful words. The cells were opened. The men came out. This was the first time the Americans had seen each other for several weeks.

Immediately they noticed that there were but three. Lieutenant George Barr was not with them. At first they were afraid that he had died. Later, however, Barr joined the group. He had been seriously ill. Two Japanese guards were helping him walk. The other three were very weak and thin, but the look of joy and happiness was seen through their hollow eyes as they greeted one another and listened to the head official again say, "The war is over. You can go home now."

The Japanese guards offered to give them a haircut. This was refused since they knew it would be a close clip to the scalp. Expecting to be back soon in America, they did not want to appear with a prisoner's haircut. They were given their old army clothes—now more than three years old—which they had been wearing when they were captured. They were then loaded on a truck and taken to a big English hotel. Everywhere they looked they saw moving crowds. Excitement prevailed. The men were fairly in a daze. At the same time they were anxious to get all the news possible. DeShazer says:

> Everyone came to look at us, and some people tried to tell us the news. So many things were happening so fast I couldn't seem to keep up with everything. After someone talked, I couldn't remember what he had said. My mind wasn't working right.

In spite of the fact that for some weeks DeShazer had been receiving better food while in prison, he thought his first meal as a free man was a wonderful treat. Like all hungry people, these half-starved men had been looking forward to eating good, rich food. Now they had their opportunity! When reporting on it, they said, "We ate all of the Irish stew that we could hold." The doctors gave them vitamin pills and shot vitamin fluid into their arms. To the satisfaction of everyone, the food they ate digested well and rapidly brought new strength.

In the open with other people, they were able quickly to get the gist of the war news. They heard about the atomic bomb. They learned that American parachute troops had flown in to rescue them. They were told the war had ended on the fifteenth of August, but, as DeShazer says, "I remembered the time God had said the victory was won." The parachute rescue group had boldly come into the Peking area. They had asked the Japanese officials where the Doolittle flyers were held. It seems the American Secret Service had been able to find out about them and their location. At the same time the Japanese officials answered their query by saying that all had been executed.

Without doubt, it will never be known exactly how word did get out that some of the Doolittle flyers, as prisoners, were still alive. DeShazer and his comrades have an interesting explanation concerning it. They think it was made possible through some U. S. Marines who had been imprisoned near them in Nanking. While in the prison there, some of the soup brought to the prisoners was in aluminum teacups. One day Lieutenant Nielson, while writing numbers on the bottom of some of these teacups, noticed that on the bottom of one was written, "U. S. Marines." Immediately Nielson made up his mind that some of the cups brought to them had at times been taken to the marines. He thought perhaps some of the cups which they were using would in turn be taken back to the marines. Lieutenant Nielson told his comrades about it, and so they picked up some nails in the yard, sharpened them on the cement walls, and started corresponding with the marines by writing on the bottoms of the aluminum teacups. Their method of corresponding was not noticed for about two months. Their plan, however, was successful, for word had gone to the marines concerning the four Doolittle flyers who were in solitary confinement.

The U. S. Marines who were in prison had been captured at the very first of the war. After several months in a prison concentration camp, they had decided to escape. Ten men tried to get away, but only three succeeded. The other seven were put into prison near the Doolittle men and were subjected to the same severe treatment except for the solitary confinement. The dishes which these marines had been using had made the rounds in the furtive correspondence.

Now that the war was over, for some reason, the marines were the first to be released. They were thus able to tell the American parachute officers that some of the Doolittle flyers were still alive. In view of this, when the Japanese officers told the parachute officers that all the Doolittle men had been executed, they knew otherwise. By putting on the pressure, the parachute men were able to find the prisoners' location and to get their release.

Following their release, the Doolittle men were now in a big hotel with many other people. These were business men and ex-policemen who had been held in concentration camps during the war. Our readers should keep in mind that the concentration camps were entirely different from the prisons where the Doolittle men had been confined. As a rule, the people in the concentration camps were quite free to move around in their confined area. Quite often they received Red Cross packages from allied countries. Some of the English policemen were greatly pleased by the kindness shown by the American Red Cross. They told the Doolittle men that the packages from the United States had the best food and were packed in such a way that nothing of significant value could have been added to the package.

The released men were given candy and concentrated foods out of some of the packages flown in by the U. S. Army. In l o o k i n g back on it, DeShazer rather humorously says:

> We would take the food that we couldn't eat and store it away in case we became hungry before mealtime. It just seemed the natural thing to do. But after a while some of the people would laugh and ask us if we were getting ready for another famine. It seemed hard to realize that we were free and would not need to suffer from hunger pangs any more.

A further instance which shows the extent to which the Doolittle flyers were thinking of food took place on the second day of their freedom. It seems that an American woman came to see the men at the Peking Hotel. She and her husband, a Frenchman who had been engaged in business in China before the war, had been in China since the opening of hostilities. This American woman said that she would like to do something for the Doolittle flyers. DeShazer says:

> She asked us what we would like. The other fellows asked me to say, so I told the lady that I could not think of anything better than a dish of ice cream. She said that was what we would get and she would make it herself. The next day we ate a freezer full of ice cream which was a real treat to us.

On the third day, American B-24s landed on the airfield of the defeated Japanese, and the next day three of the flyers were flown to Chungking. Lieutenant Barr had to stay at Peking since his health would not permit an airplane trip. At a later time he returned to America by steamship.

The wonderful news of finding four of the Doolittle flyers had been released to the world on August 20. The first word which came over the American radio that morning said that four had been found alive but did not give their names. For some hours the suspense in the heart of a little mother in Salem, Oregon, was indescribable. She had prayed and prayed. She had trusted the Lord through forty long months, but still there was an inner longing for an outward evidence that her prayers had been answered. Was it possible? would it be true that one of the four would be her own Jake? To somewhat the same degree there was a similar feeling in the heart of Helen Andrus, Jake's half-sister, who was working at that time as the secretary to the president of

Seattle Pacific College. Ears were glued to the radio anxiously waiting for further word. This further word came about noon when to the inexpressible joy of mother, stepfather, half sister, and other relatives and many, many friends, announcement was made that one of the four was Sergeant Jacob DeShazer. A dozen or more of Helen's student friends at the college locked arms with Helen and went with her to the College Chapel for a thanksgiving prayer meeting. In the home in Salem, Oregon, there was the joy of spiritual triumph and praise to the Lord.

At the same time there was deep sorrow and sympathy for others who, too, were waiting that fore-noon for a good word, only once again to be broken-hearted when they learned that their loved one was not among the four. Such was the case in the homes of Lieutenant Hallmark, Lieutenant Farrow, and the machine-gunner, Spaats, who had been so mercilessly ex-ecuted by the Japanese after six months of indescribable torture in prison; also in the homes of the bombardier and the rear gunner who drowned after the crash landing of Lieutenant Hallmark's plane off the China coast.

The great joy which came to DeShazer's mother upon learning that her son was alive and free was unbounded. It seemed that it would be impossible for anything more wonderful to take place. Imagine her added joy when word came over the air waves that Jake not only had been converted while in prison but that he had decided to give the rest of his life to missionary work. The news-paper men seemed to think this was even greater news than his deliverance from prison. Pictures of DeShazer on his knees were radioed throughout the world. Some said the young man was only seeking the limelight.

Others said it was undoubtedly a sincere statement but would be short-lived.

The released joyful flyers were flown home by way of India and across the Atlantic Ocean. As soon as De-Shazer landed in Washington, D. C., he sent word to his parents. He told them of his conversion and also of his intention to return to Japan as a missionary.

It was early in September when the party landed on American soil. They were taken immediately to the Walter Reed Hospital. As might be expected, they were subjected to many interviews with newspaper men. The released flyers soon learned that much publicity had been given to the Doolittle raid and that the public wanted to know about their prison experiences. Various newspaper men offered large sums of money for their story. DeShazer with others went to New York and spoke on "We the People" radio program. At that time DeShazer received $400 for reading one sentence over the radio. He says, "It is the most I have ever been paid for opening my mouth."

He received $2,250 from a newspaper syndicate for his personal story. He also received back pay for the forty months he had been in prison which amounted to $5,600. He says:

> I felt that I was a very wealthy person when I told Lieutenant Hite and Lieutenant Nielson goodbye and boarded an airplane in Washington, D. C., to go to the home of my parents in Salem, Oregon.

Before leaving for the West, however, a notable thing took place at a fashionable night spot in New York City. Years later this was featured in a nation-wide radio broadcast by the news commentator, Lowell Thomas. He spoke on the occasion of the eighth anniversary reunion of Doolittle's "Tokyo Raiders" at Palm Desert, California, in the spring of 1950. Mr. Thomas' tribute to De-Shazer gave testimony to the world regarding DeShazer and his stand for personal righteousness:

Sergeant DeShazer, one of the eighty original Tokyo raiders, was one of the fliers unfortunate enough to be captured by the Japanese. Three of the prisoners were executed and one starved to death. The other four went through a bitter ordeal. Then they came home after the war, and one thing that happened was a gay glittering party at New York's fashionable Stork Club. Colonel Ross Greening, pilot of the eleventh bomber in that famous take-off, was sitting beside DeShazer. They were having champagne, and Greening noticed that Jake was merely toying with his glass.

"You're not drinking," said the colonel. "How come?"

Jake thought a minute and replied, "I knew you'd ask me that, Ross, and I'll tell you about it."

"He told me," relates Greening, "how the Japs kept him in a dark cell—thirty-six months of solitary confinement—and there, day after day, week after week, he could only sit and brood. Then, one day, the black hole was filled suddenly with brilliant light. And Jake heard a voice telling him that it should be his mission to teach the Japanese how to treat human beings decently. The light and the voice were a command, bidding him to do his bit in bringing Christianity to the Japanese." Greening's own impression was deepened and confirmed by a fellow prisoner of DeShazer in that Japanese jail. The two had long discussions of DeShazer's experience and did much to convince the other Doolittle fliers of the depth and meaning of it.

Jake DeShazer resolved to become a missionary to Japan. He studied at Seattle Pacific College and went to spread the gospel in the country which had treated him so badly. Greening told of huge crowds who have heard Jake preach in Japan. In all of his work, he has had the support of his Doolittle buddies, and now the raiders have voted to support DeShazer's mission in Japan. That was the "main objective" at the 1950 reunion of the men who electrified the Allied cause and blasted the Japanese capital eight years ago.

Such experiences brought DeShazer face to face with life decisions. He states that while flying across America to the West Coast, the Lord spoke to him very definitely regarding his own life and conduct. Here it was that he promised God never again to touch alcohol or tobacco. He says, "I felt an urge to get busy with the work that God had called me to do."

Great was the joy to Jake and to the entire family when he finally reached home at Salem, Oregon. At this family altar he had heard prayer as a lad and during the years of his youth. Here also during his absence prayers had been ascending in his behalf.

As a matter of fact the Bible had been read and prayer had been offered every morning in that home since Jake had dropped out of sight. Through sympathy and interest many friends of the parents had joined them in prayer. Now great was the rejoicing. Family prayer was continued in the home, but another member had been added. Jake remembered the earlier days when he had heard the Bible read and they had met for family worship. He remembered in his early youth how he rebelled against this daily activity, but how different it was now on his return! Friends had gathered at the home and were present at the time of the morning worship. One very close friend was Mrs. J. R. Stewart. Jake, on his knees, listened with others while his parents and this guest prayed. When they had finished Jake tried to pray but he says, "Though I tried real hard, I couldn't get the praise I felt in my heart to come out in words."

After the prayer service when they stood up, Jake told the others that he wished that he could pray as they did. They encouraged him and explained that in due time he would have no difficulty in being able to pray.

It is easy to visualize what took place in that home during the next few days. There was much joy and a constant spirit of thanksgiving. Along with this was the desire to see Jake, who was nearly starved, brought back to normal physical condition. Like any mother, Mrs. Andrus spent much time in preparing good food. Nothing was spared in an effort to provide wholesome, appetizing, and enjoyable meals. The first twenty days he was out of prison he gained an average of one pound a day.

When Jake had left home in 1940 for Army service, his people were living at Madras, Oregon. They had felt, however, that they should retire from the farm and had moved to Salem, Oregon. Jake was anxious to go back to the old home town at Madras. He made such a trip and great was the celebration held in his honor. He was given a watch and asked to make a speech. He says with real meaning:

> It was a good place to begin my speech-making so I told as much as I could about the prison and about the salvation I had received when I read the Bible. I ran out of wind pretty fast. I was sweating and working harder than I had ever worked in my life. It seems funny now, but I was nearly thirty-three years old, and this was my first public speech. In bed alone that night I prayed to God. I felt comfort from Him and a promise of victory if I would continue to try.

On his return trip to Salem, he was given two more opportunities to speak. One of these was at a youth rally where Dr. Nathan Cohen Beskin, a converted Russian

Jew, was the main speaker. He spoke again at an Evangelical Church. Without doubt these experiences were of great help to DeShazer since it assisted him in putting himself on record and strengthening his commitment to God. He admitted that it was getting easier to speak. Still speech making continued to be a real task and somewhat of a cross.

He was supposed to have been given a ninety-day leave from the Army. For some unknown reason, however, within two weeks after arriving home he received a telegram asking him to report to the Santa Ana Air Base in California. After reporting there he immediately asked for a discharge from the Army. To his surprise he was informed that it would be impossible to get out for some time since there was a large number of soldiers to be discharged.

Not having anything to do and having essential freedom, he did considerable visiting around Santa Ana. This was of particular interest since he had several relatives in that area. He was called upon to speak at various church and youth services. At one church someone asked him if he had ever been baptized. He responded that he had been baptized but not publicly. He recalled that while he was in prison he had wished that he could be baptized. He also recalled that at that time in rather strange simplicity he had actually gone over to one side of his prison cell where the wind was blowing the water from the eaves through the window and had stood in this spattering rain and praised God for a water baptism. He remembers this experience with much joy. He is thankful to these Christian friends for their zeal and their help to his Christian faith.

While he was at Santa Ana, a military blunder was

committed by a leading official. This received nation-
wide publicity. There happened to be some fifty soldiers
in this particular camp who had been prisoners of war.
One of the most outstanding was DeShazer himself. Here
was a man just released from the nightmare of solitary
confinement, devastating disease, and semi-starvation.
For no known reason he was told to report for K. P.
duty. He was assigned to cleaning dishes. While he was
in the act of carrying dishes, a newspaper man came in
and without authorization took DeShazer's picture as he,
weak and emaciated, was carrying a large tray of dishes.
This picture appeared in one of the leading Los Angeles
papers. Naturally, it aroused a great deal of public senti-
ment against the military authorities for putting De-
Shazer and other former prisoners of war at menial
tasks. The officials responsible for the blunder were given
a reprimand. As a result, DeShazer was sent immediately
to a hospital for further observation and care. It also re-
sulted in stepping up the effort in getting a discharge.
Just before he was sent to the hospital, he was called in
to see the commanding officer who admitted that it had
been a great mistake for him to be put on K.P. duty.
The commanding officer also told him that he would do
everything possible to help. Again DeShazer was made
to praise the Lord for this further evidence of the guiding
hand of his Heavenly Father.

CHAPTER XIII

BEGINS MISSIONARY TRAINING COURSE

DeShazer had finished his high school work in May, 1931. To anyone having been out of school fourteen years, it would be a real test of courage and determination to return again to the class room. Add to this the experiences of several years in the Army and more than three years in prison without books or reading, and it is difficult to imagine the handicap confronting DeShazer in attempting to carry out his plan to train for missionary service.

Things, however, were moving very rapidly in his life. The fact that he had announced through the news reports his intention to train to go back to Japan as a missionary brought literature and catalogs from dozens of colleges and schools from all parts of America. His sister, Helen, was a student at Seattle Pacific College. This provided a natural open door in that direction. Then, too, Helen was secretary to President Watson. She had gone to the new home of her parents in Salem, Oregon, to greet Jake. Under date of September 13, 1945, she wrote to President Watson:

> My brother reached home about midnight last night. You can well imagine that there is not a happier home in the world than ours. He looks better than we had feared—has gained some fifteen pounds since being rescued. The most wonderful part of all, of course, is his experience with God and desire to return to Japan as a missionary after proper training. We are anxious to hear from his own lips what the news stories have said about

Home Again
DeShazer and comrades arriving in
Washington, D. C.

Supremely Happy
Mother now knows for sure her Jake
is alive.

"It Tastes so Good!"
DeShazer gets all the fried chicken
he can eat.

Back with Family
Jake with mother, stepfather and
sister, Helen.

Picture Story of DeShazer's Rapid Recovery

When First Released

Two Weeks Later

Three Weeks Later

Six Months Later

God's communing with him during his time in solitary confinement.

Naturally, I am hoping that S. P. C. will be his choice of a college, but we will be happy with whatever decision he makes.

A few days later she wrote:

Will you please send an application blank to my brother, Jacob? He wants to start at the beginning of the autumn quarter. We shall ask the school authorities at Madras, Oregon, to send his high school transcript. I encouraged him to wait until the winter quarter but he would rather get started even though he will not be discharged from the Army until the middle of December. He will be on furlough until then. I trust all the details can be worked out. Thank you.

On September 17, Vice-President Otto M. Miller of Seattle Pacific College wrote DeShazer in part as follows:

Welcome back to the United States and the Pacific Northwest once more. We are certainly glad you are home again, and hope you will get your discharge from the Army very soon. The sacrifices you have made have been most severe, but we pray the years have not been in vain.

We feel almost personally acquainted with you through our contact with Helen. Believe me, you had one excited and happy little sister the day the Associated Press called and said you had been released.

We are so glad to learn that you met the Lord while you were confined and that you expect to go into His service. Your testimony that has gone out over the radio and in the papers will have untold influence for good.

We do not know your plans in regard to preparing for this future work, but if they include Seattle Pacific College we shall be very happy, indeed. I believe you will find here the type of training and environment that will be most helpful to you after the experiences you have had. . . . also, we shall allow you credit toward graduation for the training you received in the Army.

This letter is not to high pressure you or to rush you into a decision, but merely to let you know how glad we are that you are back and to extend to you a welcome to Seattle Pacific College should it fit in with your desires. In case your plans do not include Seattle Pacific be assured our interest in you is just as sincere and our good wishes for your future just as genuine. May the Lord guide you into every good way and bring you true success.

On September 20, President Charles Hoyt Watson of Seattle Pacific College wrote in part:

Dear Jacob: I trust you will allow me to address you by your first name; since Helen has been my secretary this summer, I have come to feel very close to you. As indicated in Professor Miller's letter the other day, we greatly appreciate what you and your comrades have done. I am sure God now has a plan whereby you can use the tragic experiences of the last forty months for the uplift and salvation of many. We pray God's blessing upon you as you go forward in fellowship with the Lord.

I have just received a card from Helen indicating your desire for an application blank from the school. She indicated you were anxious to get started immediately with your school program. Be assured of our willingness and desire to cooperate in every way. If possible, it would be splendid for you to be here by Friday morning, September 28. The program of that day and of Saturday, the 29th, will make it possible for our teachers to give you better advice in regard to enrollment.

In the midst of conflicting desires and varied advices, DeShazer was not exactly sure what to do. Part of the time he thought he would wait until after he was discharged from the Army before starting to school. As he now looks back on developments, he says that the Lord led in a wonderful way. Calls were coming in from various sections of the West for him to come as a speaker. One of these calls was from North Central Washington at Okanogan where the Reverend Finkbeiner was pastor. This man had been a good friend of DeShazer years before at Madras, Oregon. DeShazer accepted this invitation and while making the trip stopped off at Seattle Pacific College to visit his sister, Helen, who had returned to her work in President Watson's office.

As would be expected Helen introduced her brother to the president of the college. DeShazer describes this brief interview:

> President Watson asked me when I was going to start to school. I said I didn't think I could go to school before the winter quarter, but he gave me a good chance to start immediately if I so desired. The result was that the next day I started to college.

Thus it was that approximately two months after DeShazer had been released from prison he was back in school again. Would he be able to make the necessary adjustments? Would he be able once again to get down to study? Would he be able to meet the requirements for missionary preparation and service? Should he have taken more time to get adjusted and regain his health? These and many other questions constantly came to mind. The long experiences in prison already were beginning to seem like a dream, but the experiences of the last two months seemed equally unreal. Speaking of this he says:

> Think of it! Only three months before the time I started to school I had been seriously ill and thought I was going to die. God had healed me from sickness, baptized me with the Holy Spirit, and provided everything I needed in preparing to become a missionary. How im-

possible it had all seemed to me, but all God asked me
to do was to try, and then He worked. The government
was paying all of my tuition and was giving me subsis-
tence money. I was free to give my full time to study.
I felt as if God had brought me to school.

The change from prison life to a life of freedom was
tremendous. The change from a life of idleness to one of
activity brought new ambition, but with it the taxing of
his entire physical energy. The shift from introspection
and mental apathy to one of study and intellectual activity
required almost a miracle. The greatest shift, however,
in many ways was that from an environment completely
out of line with Christian life and godliness to the atmosphere and optimism of a Christian college campus.

Without doubt many schools of America would have
duplicated for this new Christian student the same experiences which he had at Seattle Pacific College. Perhaps
it will not be violating any ethical standard to state
some of the experiences and feelings which he had as he
entered this completely new type of environment:

> I was staying in the men's residence hall and was en-
> couraged a great deal by the other fellows who were my
> companions. I was older than most of them, but no one
> seemed to notice. I could not help admiring young men
> who had found the Lord and were going to make the
> most of their lives by following Jesus.
>
> The young people of Seattle Pacific College were the
> finest people with whom I had ever been associated. After
> my war experience, I felt as if I had come in from a
> howling wind-storm into a good strong house. These
> young people had no craving for the world. They knew
> the Christian way of holiness. They had experienced the
> cleansing power of God in their lives. I could see living
> examples of what the Holy Spirit taught me in prison.
> Many denominations were represented, but there was one

faith and wonderful harmony of spirit. Then, too, there were students from many countries.

The faculty men and women were Spirit-filled. They knew the Bible. They could give splendid instruction and wise counsel. I never realized before coming to this college that God had so many people who were so nearly perfect in their lives. They had the same idea that God had given me. This wonderful spirit delivers from willful, disobedient sin. In Jesus there is perfect love toward God and toward our fellow men.

I received fine spiritual guidance at S. P. C. I was able to have a closer walk with God as I was taught to read the Bible and pray to Jesus. Many of us learned Bible verses so that we could better tell others of the hope that was in us. I found that memorizing Scripture had been one of the greatest aids in helping me to have greater faith and a closer walk with the Lord. Our teachers encouraged us in every means of grace available, such as singing gospel songs, reading the Bible, giving testimonies, memorizing Scripture, praying and associating with other Christians.

DeShazer was open-minded and very anxious to learn. He was constantly comparing the Bible teaching through his further study with his prison experience. The way he summarizes his conclusions along this line is profound through its simplicity:

The Spirit of Jesus is the Holy Spirit. When we have become Christians, the Holy Spirit comes and dwells in our hearts. Most sincere Christians experience a baptism with the Holy Spirit if they seek a closer walk with God. John the Baptist while preaching the gospel had baptized with water, but he foretold the coming of Jesus. John was the forerunner of Jesus, and he had said of the Christ: "He that cometh after me is mightier than I, whose shoes I am not worthy to bear: he shall baptize you with the Holy Ghost and with fire" (Matt. 3:11).

This baptism usually comes, when the believer is fully

consecrated to God by such a sincere and honest love
that he desires to please God in everything that he does.
"Whether therefore ye eat, or drink, or whatsoever ye do,
do all to the glory of God" (I Cor. 10:31). When a person conscientiously tries to please God in all his life,
the baptism with the Holy Spirit can be expected. This
baptism is "of power, and of love, and of a sound mind"
(II Tim. 1:7). The Spirit of Jesus dwelling in us
quickens and enlivens us to the things of God. The baptism with the Holy Spirit is greatly to be desired, and
after it is attained, the desire for sin is gone.

Those who have been baptized with the Holy Spirit are
still human beings. They may err in judgment and
make mistakes, and their bodies may become sick with
disease. However, the intent of the heart is always to
love God and other people. They will quickly turn away
from those things which are evil or have the appearance
of evil. They are content with the things that they have,
and they will not knowingly do anything that is displeasing to the Lord. A fuller realization of God's presence is
always appreciated by those who have experienced the
baptism with the Holy Spirit.

The Bible teaches people to live holy lives. It is
known that God hates sin and that holiness is a way of
living which is free from willful disobedience. We are not
able to live so in our own strength, but God is able to
make us stand and to deliver us from unrighteousness.
I did not know about these teachings when I was in
prison, but I know that I was baptized with the Holy
Spirit and that a great flood of love came into my heart
when this experience took place. I have often marveled
at the way this baptism came to me and the way that
God led me to a believing group of people even before
I had a realization of its full significance.

Very soon after beginning his school work in the
autumn of 1945, DeShazer was being called to so many
points as a featured speaker that it almost disrupted his
school program. Requests came from hundreds of miles

away agreeing to pay expenses and an honorarium if he would come and give his testimony. In order properly to protect him provision was made whereby the field secretary of Seattle Pacific College, the Reverend George T. Klein, took charge of his schedule. A special leaflet was prepared setting forth some of the highlights of De-Shazer's experience. Mr. Klein and DeShazer made on the average about three trips per week to hold public services in which the former Japanese prisoner was the featured speaker.

DeShazer's parents for many years had been members of the Free Methodist Church. It was not long before DeShazer himself was identified with this denomination. He felt that this church was definitely Bible-centered and advocated complete separation from sin and the world, and also that it stressed the need and glorious possibility of living a Spirit-filled life. Because it was very obvious that he was looking toward the life of a minister and missionary, his church granted him a "local preacher's" license which is the first step in the Methodist tradition in preparing to become an ordained minister.

Over and over again, DeShazer expressed appreciation for the double advantage he found at Seattle Pacific College. In his own words, these advantages were "Full recognition of academic work leading to a degree and the right kind of spiritual guidance which is of more value than anything else in the world."

He was revelling in his associations. He enjoyed being with the other fellows, mixing with the various groups in the college cafeteria, participating in the public services, the various student prayer meetings and other extra-curricular activities. He bought an automobile and was frequently taking other students to various Christian services, particularly where he was to participate. At times, however, he was ready to let others know something of his experiences and also some of his inner problems :

> It was a great change from the life I had been living in a Japanese war prison. Everyone on the campus called me "Jake." It seemed that they all knew me since my name and pictures had been in the papers. I tried to remember the other students' names, but it seemed difficult to remember all of them. However, they were all my friends, and I enjoyed their friendship very much.

He was greatly interested in his speaking engagements. At the same time he felt a great urge to accelerate his school program as much as possible. As his first year of school moved along and he learned there would be a summer session, he made plans to complete his total four-year college course in three calendar years. Since the government was paying all of his expenses and since he had a modest bank account, he really wanted for nothing. Such were his plans early in 1946. These plans, however, were intensified and given much more meaning after he began to share his desires and plans with a lovely Christian young woman, also a student at Seattle Pacific College.

CHAPTER XIV

JAKE AND FLORENCE—ROMANCE
AND MARRIAGE

Early in the spring of 1946 DeShazer went to a Youth for Christ service with Miss Florence Matheny. This young lady, a few years younger than DeShazer, was a junior in college. She had come to Seattle Pacific in the fall of 1945, from Toddville, Iowa, after completing her first two years at Lenox Junior College. Notwithstanding the fact that one was a freshman and the other a junior, this couple was often seen together. As might be expected they felt a common purpose. In describing her, DeShazer in retrospect says:

> She was a very attractive young lady, the most attractive young lady I had ever met, and she wanted to go into full-time work for the Lord. We both felt a oneness of purpose, and, when I asked Miss Matheny if she would marry me, she said that she would. When we prayed to Jesus, we felt that He would be pleased to give us a life together.

It was a great joy to these two fine Christian young people to be together in a Christian college. During his first year, DeShazer demonstrated his positive interest in basic training for a major in missions by choosing standard lower division required courses. His subjects for this first year were as follows: English Composition, Fundamentals of Speech, Introduction to Philosophy, Literary Backgrounds, Advanced Algebra, Personal Evangelism, Gospel of Mark, Survey of Old Testament Prophets,

Church Polity and Doctrine, Speech, Book of Psalms, Piano, and Choral Singing. During the summer of 1946 he took such other courses as Economics of the Present Social Order, Principles of Sociology, and Survey of Biological Science.

In spite of the handicap under which he was operating, it should be said that from the very outset he was able to do good if not superior work. As a matter of fact, throughout his entire school work he failed in but one short course (and that because of too many speaking engagements) and received only two "D" grades. His final grade score was 2.28.

At the close of the summer school in 1946, Jake and Florence went to Gresham, Oregon, where on August 29, they were married. The ceremony was performed by Florence's former pastor, the Reverend J. K. French. Much publicity was given to this event which took place approximately one year after DeShazer's release from prison. Over and over again he was known to say that he felt God was fulfilling his promise as found in Prov. 3:6, "In all thy ways acknowledge him, and he shall direct thy paths." Jake and Florence felt this was definitely true in connection with their courtship and marriage. They felt God had directed them in finding one another. Now the two went forward together with plans to tell the true God-given plan of salvation.

The next day after they were married, they started in their 1940 Pontiac for Toddville, Iowa. Florence evidently wanted to take her bridegroom back to the old home town perhaps so that some of her former suitors might see him. Whatever the reason she found great joy in making the trip.

On the way they stopped from place to place to hold

meetings. On the second day they were in Boise, Idaho.
Here Florence and Jake carried out a schedule that had
been arranged previously by the Reverend George T.
Klein. All the way to Toddville, while there, and on
their return, they were able to greet many friends of the
past and make new ones. The entire trip took a full
month.

Jake admits that he was "almost taken off his feet"
when he first made a date with Florence. But, let us forget Jake himself for a time and get better acquainted
with this fine young lady. She was twenty-five years old
at the time of their marriage. She is the daughter of Mr.
and Mrs. A. J. Matheny of Toddville, Iowa. Florence
has blue eyes and dark brown hair. She was born in
Marion, Iowa, August 9, 1921. One of her earliest recol-
lections is going to Sunday school. She reports that on
one particular Sunday morning on a cold winter day in
January with wind and snow outside she remembers
joining heartily with other boys and girls in the primary class in singing "Jesus loves me, This I know."

As the years came and went, Florence, like any other
healthy girl, continued to grow and enjoy life and that to
the full. She romped and played and was alert to everything taking place. She greatly enjoyed visits of missionaries to the little village church. Her school work was
easy. She was little more than thirteen years old when
she entered the Monroe Township High School at Toddville. She graduated in 1938 with a grade score of 3.00.

Then things began to change. Throughout her high
school days she had come to think more and more of what
she would do later on in life. Unfortunately, thoughts of
the church and Christian service as a career became dim.
In particular, she felt she wanted to be a school teacher.

Along with this was a growing desire for pleasure and adventure.

So it was that as a very attractive girl of seventeen years she left the little village of Toddville and went away to college. She entered the Lenox Junior College at Hopkinton, Iowa, in the fall of 1938. Here life was just too full of activity to allow much time for either study or devotions. The usual young girl courtships were numerous in the life of this freshman girl. Once again, however, we see the influence of early training and of God's care. Florence admits that her mother's prayers and her early training kept her from going into out-broken sin to the extent that many of her classmates did. Yet she says, "My heart was as black as any of theirs for I, too, failed to accept Jesus Christ as my Saviour."

The summer of 1939 came, and she entered her sophomore year. Being still bent on becoming a school teacher, she was holding herself rather definitely to the required course for certification. During those months on various occasions she came face to face with the demands of the gospel. She had various opportunities to give herself to the Lord, but for some reason continued to reject extended mercy and to say, "No," to the invitations. Various tragedies in connection with other students and in the community caused her heart to be stirred. Time after time she came near to the point of decision but finally backed down for fear of what her friends would say. More than that there seemed to be deep seated in her mind the thought that she would have to make a definite break with worldly friendships and accept a real life of dedication to the call of God if she actually surrendered to the Lord's will. This she was unwilling to do.

On June 2, 1940, she finished her junior college work receiving her diploma and completing the requirements for teacher certification. Her first school was in her home community where she began as a rural school teacher in August, 1940. Without doubt, this changed the whole course of her future life, for it brought her back to the little home Sunday school where once again she felt the influence of kind friends and the ministry of the gospel of the Lord Jesus Christ. Because of a shortage of Sunday-school workers, she was asked to take the office of secretary. She accepted this responsibility, but owing to rebellion in her heart against the Lord, she would not stay to the morning preaching service after the adjournment of the Sunday school. This situation continued for a whole year.

Conditions, however, changed in August of 1941. The new pastor who had recently come to the church was very friendly. Both he and his wife took an unusual interest in young people and particularly in Florence. This new pastor seemed to understand Florence, and in a very real way won her confidence.

When a leading evangelist was announced for a special evangelistic series in a neighboring city, this young pastor persuaded Florence with several other young people to attend an evening service. When they arrived, they found the church already filled and people standing near the door. The only available seats were those in the very front row.

The evangelist brought a stirring message which seemed to bring conviction to many of those present. There was a definite call for those wanting to seek the Lord to come forward. Quickly the altar was lined with seekers. Florence, however, still more or less cynical in her attitude was able to brush aside the appeal of the sermon and joined only passively in the invitation songs. She was even somewhat amused at the entire proceedings.

While she was in this more or less careless state of mind, someone slipped to her side and said, "Wouldn't you like to be a Christian?" She turned quickly and saw that it was her pastor. The tone of his voice and the expression on his face disarmed Florence completely. Beyond the invitation of the pastor she seemed to hear the very voice of Christ say, "Come unto Me and I will give you rest." She reports that there had been a deep-seated longing in her heart for soul rest. At this time she became very conscious of this longing and was aware of her great need for a Saviour. She dropped on her knees right where she was and began to pray. Various workers gathered around and began to encourage her in her effort. In describing the experience Florence says:

> I made an honest effort to pray but no words came. I was thankful then that the Bible says, "A broken and a contrite heart, O God, thou wilt not despise." Then, "Likewise the Spirit also helpeth our infirmities; for we know not what we should pray for as we ought: but the Spirit itself maketh intercession for us with groanings which cannot be uttered." When I arose from my knees, the weight of sin was gone, and a new song was in my heart, for I had decided to follow Jesus no matter what the cost.

That was a lifelong decision which over and over Florence recalls with great joy. But the days that followed were real testing days. The Lord had forgiven her, but on the condition that she make restitution for her wrong acts. She had promised the Lord to take up her cross and follow Him. In spite of the opposition and the obstacles which Satan seemed to throw across her path, she was able to carry out her vows to make necessary restitution. She did ask forgiveness of others and moved forward in the will of the Lord. One of the most significant ways she was able to take up her cross was in her little one-room schoolhouse where she would have prayer with her pupils. During those days she had a consciousness of the leadership and blessing of the Holy Spirit.

As weeks and months came and went and as Florence studied the Word of God and analyzed her own heart, she gradually came to realize there were those things in her life which were not pleasing to the Lord. She also seemed to think there was greater victory for her each day over temptation. Here is her testimony in this connection:

> I knew that although my sins were forgiven, yet deep within my innermost being there still lurked the carnal sins of pride, jealousy, and anger. In June, 1942, I attended a tent meeting near my home, and one night while kneeling there in the straw by a little wooden bench, I asked the Lord to create within me a clean heart. God answered my prayer and cleansed my heart from sin. Life became sweet, and my days were filled with happy service for the Lord.

Not long after this experience her pastor preached a message on the "Unequal yoke," and Florence was led along with others to make a real vow before the Lord never to marry a man who was not a Christian. Such a decision for Florence as well as for many a young woman in a small community was serious. She did not know whether she would ever be able to move away from this community into a larger one. Practically every young man she knew, however splendid and fine he seemed to be, was not a follower of the Lord Jesus Christ.

For some three years this fine Christian young woman continued to work faithfully in the Sunday school, attending preaching services, and promoting the Lord's kingdom in every way possible. She was keeping herself separate from the world and open for the leadership of the Lord. Then came the summer of 1945. The Lord showed her that there was still a deeper consecration to be made. This specific call also came during a tent meeting. The Lord came in a very definite way and revealed to Florence that he wanted her not only for full-time service but for missionary service. The path seemed to be very clear. It meant to discontinue public school teaching, separate herself from home and family and enter a missionary training school. She says the Lord very definitely led her to Seattle Pacific College.

Between the time of this special call from God and actually arriving on the campus of Seattle Pacific College to take up her further school work, Florence had a most unusual experience. It seems that almost by chance she picked up a newspaper and saw an article and a picture of one of "Jimmy" Doolittle's flyers who had spent forty months in a Japanese prison camp and had found the Lord as his personal Saviour. The article went on to say that this former prisoner of war wanted to return to Japan as a missionary and that he was planning to attend some Christian college. "What a coincidence it would be," Florence thought, "if he should choose the same college that I have chosen. Perhaps I might even get to shake hands with him. Who knows?"

We now know the sequel to this thought. Florence came to Seattle Pacific College and entered on her train-

McKinley Auditorium at Seattle Pacific College
Where for three years DeShazer attended daily Chapel and frequently gave his testimony.

Study! Study!! Study!!!
Completed full college course in
three calendar years.

At Youth for Christ
Jake gives testimony with Bob Pierce
as master of ceremonies.

First Year in College
DeShazer had full schedule of study, devotion, public speaking, athletics and romance

Second Year in College
Married Florence Matheny. Both go forward with college program.
They study Japanese together.

Last Year in College
Jake and Florence happy together in college housing unit. Little Paul arrives.

ing course. She says that at the beginning of that college
year in the fall of 1945, the Lord gave a special verse
from the first chapter of Philippians, "Being confident of
this very thing, that he which hath begun a good work
in you will perform it until the day of Jesus Christ."

Not only did she get to shake hands with the Doolittle flyer, but also within a year she became his wife. It
meant, of course, that Jake moved out of the men's resi-
dence hall. He had made careful plans for this several
months before, for his name had been upon the waiting list
for one of the veterans' housing units which was under
the control of the college.

In this new relationship, Jake and Florence found
great joy and delight. They shared in their responsibil-
ities of the home, including the cooking. Jake, however,
was carrying the greater school load since he was now
only a second quarter sophomore and Florence was almost a senior. It was at this time that both of them began studying Japanese with Professor Bokko Tsuchiyama. (It is of particular interest to note that this
Japanese teacher returned to Japan a year in advance of
the DeShazers and that today Tsuchiyama is principal of
the Christian college in Tokyo of which DeShazer is now
a trustee and instructor.)

The calls for DeShazer to go on speaking engagements were just as numerous as during the year before.
Now, however, Florence went along for many of these
meetings. The two young people seemed to get along in
a wonderful way. Jake's message of love based upon his
prison experiences and Florence's message of consecration to missionary endeavor seemed to touch the hearts
and minds of every audience. People enjoyed having
them in their homes. Youth groups enjoyed their testi-

monies. Many were the decisions for Christ, and many
were the dedications to missionary service.

When at home, they read the Bible and prayed together at least twice every day. Over and over they
emphasized the value of their little family altar. They
said they had dedicated their time, their strength, and
their possessions to the Lord.

In addition to intensive study of the Japanese language,
DeShazer continued his basic training in liberal arts.
Along with further piano lessons he pursued such sub-
jects as Principles of Sermon Preparation, Social Prob-
lems, Survey of Christian Doctrine, History of the Chris-
tian Church, Physical Science, The British Empire, The
Epistle to the Hebrews, and Religious Audio and Visual
Aids.

A new experience came to DeShazer on the last day
of October, 1947. He attended his classes but seemed
to be living out of this world. Other students greeted
him with congratulations and this big question mark, "Is
it a boy or a girl?" It was not long, however, until
everyone knew that the new baby, born at 8:30 that
morning, was a bouncing eight-pound-seven-ounce boy
and the very image of his mother.

DeShazer announced that they were going to call the
lad Paul Edward, with the further statement "The Paul
is after the disciple Paul, and I don't know where the
Edward came from." The dad was rather free in the
distribution of candy bars.

Between visits to the hospital DeShazer was trying to
study and attend classes. For the first time, however,
he was spending his evenings alone at the veterans' unit
at 2585 Third Avenue West, just about six blocks up the
hill from the college. He admitted he had a lot of time

for study but made the further comment that, "It is rather hard to concentrate."

From that time on DeShazer was a typical doting dad. Seldom could he make a public statement without telling something about his boy, Paul, and it was rather difficult to get a picture of him alone without the baby.

During the remainder of the school year Florence stayed at home to take care of Paul. She had only eight credits more of school work in order to finish her Bachelor of Arts Degree. Since Jake himself would have to go to school the following summer, they agreed to finish their work together during the summer session.

CHAPTER XV
COLLEGE GRADUATION—TOUR ACROSS
CONTINENT—OFF TO JAPAN

By special dispensation on the part of the college faculty, Jake and Florence were allowed to go through the regular graduation exercises in June even though it was necessary for both of them to do further work subsequently in the summer session. Graduation day, June 7, 1948, was to this fine missionary couple a memorable day. As Jake and Florence walked across the platform in McKinley Auditorium to receive their diplomas and congratulations from the President of Seattle Pacific College, they paused while President Watson made the following statement:

And now it is my great pleasure to honor our best known student, Jacob DeShazer, together with his wife, Florence.

It was a little over six years ago on April 18, 1942, to be exact, that Sergeant DeShazer as a member of General "Jimmy" Doolittle's squadron made the first raid on Japan. Jake was one of several members of this squadron who were unreported for more than three years. The hearts of many in addition to those of his immediate family were greatly concerned and world-wide interest was aroused when, soon after the cessation of hostilities, the radio announcement went around the world that Sergeant Jacob DeShazer was one of four still alive. Freedom came on that memorable August 20, 1945, after he had spent forty months in a Japanese prison, most of the time in solitary confinement.

The record of his remarkable conversion while in prison

after the reading of the Word of God has produced a profound impression on the entire Christian world. What has been even more remarkable, however, is his decision at that time and his consistent purpose in carrying out that decision to give himself to the ministry of the gospel among the Japanese, the very people who had so persecuted him. The record of that decision in tract form in the Japanese language has already been the means of the conversion of thousands upon thousands of Japanese people.

His decision to train for Christian missionary service brought him to the campus of Seattle Pacific College. It was here he met Florence Matheny. Together they have carried on their study of the Japanese language and pursuit of the regular college program and indeed the establishment of a home. They expect to complete their work for the degree during the coming summer session. It is a high point in the history of Seattle Pacific College and a most enjoyable day in my life to confer upon Jacob and Florence the degree of Bachelor of Arts from Seattle Pacific College.

Following the formal graduation, things moved very rapidly with respect to the DeShazers. They had already been accepted as out-going missionaries to Japan by the Missionary Board of the Free Methodist Church of North America. Many calls came for them in this connection to do deputation work, to meet with various groups and make definite plans for going to the Orient. Many other groups, including Youth for Christ, young people's summer camps, the Bible Meditation League, church conferences and others were sending in calls for them. In addition to this, of course, was a full summer school schedule for Jake and a partial summer session load for Florence. A niece of Jake, Elaine Blackwell, assisted in caring for little Paul. This summer school work, however, was done with high acceptability. During the last four quarters of his course, DeShazer had continued his study of the Japanese language and had completed such courses as The Gospel of John, Romans, The Epistles of Peter and John, Christian Philosophy, Pauline Epistles, Youth Work in the Church, Life of Christ, Advanced Homiletics, Church and Pastoral Administration, The Revelation, Psychology, and Introduction to Christian Education. Thus, in three calendar years, he had completed a regular four-year college course including nine credits through military training, a total of one hundred eighty-six quarter credits. He received the Bachelor of Arts degree with a Major in Missions. Florence also received the Bachelor of Arts degree with a Major in Missions.

It was now almost the first of September, and the couple was hoping to sail soon after the first of November. The maritime strike, however, made it impossible for them to sail until December 14. This extra month gave them opportunity to make better arrangements for their trip. Jake visited Winona Lake, Indiana, where he conferred with his missionary secretary, Dr. Byron S. Lamson, General Secretary of the Free Methodist Missionary Board. There he was able to learn more about the splendid foundation work which had been laid by this Board throughout many years in Japan.

For an eight-day period in September, Jake and Florence had charge of one of the booths at the Third World Missions Conference, which was held on the campus of Seattle Pacific College. About one hundred missionaries were present to participate in this conference. Between fifty and sixty different missions and missionary boards were represented.

At the conclusion of the Conference, the little family started on a speaking tour of the United States. This was somewhat of an eye opener for Jake, for he found there was great enthusiasm throughout America for promoting Christian missions in Japan. There seemed to be a feeling everywhere that the doors of Japan are open wide to the gospel. They toured east and then south and returned west to Los Angeles and San Francisco.

Here they boarded the *U. S. S. General Meigs* and left San Francisco, December 14, 1948, just six years and eight months after he had gone on the *U. S. S. Hornet* under the Golden Gate Bridge, April 2, 1942. Almost exactly half of the intervening time he had spent in prison. The *General Meigs* was a rough riding ship. There was a total of sixteen people in the cabin where Florence and Paul stayed. Most of these other people were missionaries. These included Miss Alice Fensome, another Free Methodist missionary, who was making her first trip to Japan.

The ship docked for a day or two at Honolulu thus making it possible for the DeShazers to meet the parents of several students they had known in college. They spoke at one of the churches, for one of the docking days was Sunday. They left the Honolulu harbor Sunday night. A large crowd gathered and sang gospel songs as the boat pulled away.

While making this two-week trip, DeShazer, of course, had many thoughts. Some of these he has written down:

> This time I was not going as a bombardier, but I was going as a missionary. Now I had love and good intentions toward Japan. How much better it is to go out to conquer evil with the gospel of peace! The strength and power must come from God, but God's promise is, "I have set before thee an open door, and no man can shut it" (Rev. 3:8). I have tried God's promises out in the past, and God always keeps his promises.

My brave little wife was ready for the fight. There might be hardship and trouble, but there would be no turning back on her part. This is God's battle and God says, "Be not afraid nor dismayed by reason of this great multitude: for the battle is not yours, but God's" (II Chron. 20:15). To fight with God gives confidence and victory, and the victory will be glorious. People who find Jesus are never sorry. Jesus gives a better life in this world and the sure promise of eternal joy in the next. We are going to Japan to tell about Jesus and show the way of peace and happiness. We hope to see Japan become a Christian nation that Japan may be among the nations that have the joy of worshiping before the true God.

CHAPTER XVI

FIRST EXPERIENCES AS MISSIONARY

More than one million tracts concerning the Doolittle raider who turned missionary had been distributed throughout Japan. This tract in Japanese contained a blank to be signed by those who would accept Jesus Christ as their Saviour. Many thousands of these were signed and returned. In view of this the name, DeShazer, was known to many Japanese people. So it was that on December 28, 1948, when DeShazer and his little family arrived at the Yokohama docks crowds were waiting to see them. Many were anxious to know the cause of the change of attitude of a man who had been held for many months by the Japanese in a solitary cell. They could not understand how one's heart once filled with animosity could now be overflowing with love for his persecutors.

As they pressed around DeShazer and asked many questions, he felt at first quite helpless. He knew he had been "born again," but he also knew that an expression like that meant very little to people who did not know the Bible. It did not take long, however, for him to commit the problem to the Lord. He says:

By myself I was helpless. For flesh and blood cannot reveal the great spiritual truths. It is God that reveals and saves, and we must have God's forgiving, tender spirit in order for God to use us. If God will use us, even children can understand, and people who have put their trust in man-made idols will turn from idolatry and put their trust in the true and living God.

Troubles and disappointments were not slow in coming. The DeShazers had been taken by friends to an American style house, but there was little heat in the house, and these newcomers from America felt damp and cold. The next day little Paul was ill with a bad cold. Jake had already accepted an appointment to speak at the Suginami Free Methodist Church in Tokyo on the next Sunday. The baby's cold became worse, and the house seemed to be extremely cold. By Saturday they began to look for a doctor. They finally learned that they could take Paul to an Army hospital.

Here the doctor checked the baby carefully and said he should be left at the hospital where it was warmer and where he could be given medical care. This was a hard blow to Florence. How could she leave the little fellow in the hospital and not be near him for a week! They were able, however, to commit their situation to the Lord and particularly the case of little Paul. DeShazer says:

> It was good to know Jesus at that time and to realize that he knows all about us and our every problem. When we committed our lives to Jesus, we had given everything. We would venture our lives for Jesus' sake that the precious gospel might bring peace and joy. The time of testing had come, but we must not turn back now; "No man, having put his hand to the plow, and looking back, is fit for the kingdom of God" (Luke 9:62).

A week later Florence was able to go back to the hospital and see Paul. He seemed to be improving. On this same Saturday, Jake visited two churches in Tokyo, the Suginami and the Oji. As an interpreter he had Dr. Kaneo Oda also a graduate of Seattle Pacific College.

To speak through an interpreter was a new experience for DeShazer. It was not so difficult to give his personal experience by way of testimony. It was far more difficult when he tried to give an organized discourse. Having to stop and wait for the interpreter made it very easy for him to forget his line of thought. On this occasion, however, he tried to prove that God had put his seal on the Bible as the revealed Word. He said in part:

> We have the sign of prophecy and the resurrection of Jesus Christ from the dead. These are conclusive proofs that the Bible is God's plan of salvation. Since this is true, the promise of John 1:12 will work if we meet the conditions. The condition is to receive Jesus, for the verse says: "As many as received him, to them gave he power to become the sons of God, even to them that believe on his name." We cannot save ourselves, but if we receive Jesus the power needed for salvation will come from Heaven and we become the sons of God.

It was a great joy to DeShazer to be in Japan and have the privilege of preaching the gospel. News concerning him had spread everywhere. Consequently, churches and halls were filled to capacity. DeShazer has used John 1:12 as a test many times. In this connection he asks people whether they are willing to receive Jesus. In response many hundreds are quick to indicate their decision to try out the promises of God in order that they may receive the gift of eternal life.

Conditions continued to improve for the new missionaries. They were able to transfer to a warm hotel. After a few more days, they went by train to Osaka. Here again they were able to get located in a warm hotel. The next day, Sunday, DeShazer spoke at the Nippon Bashi Church and at the Fusei Church in Osaka.

The eagerness of the people to hear him was a surprise to him. He admits that although multitudes were making decisions to become Christians, his heart was still saddened because of the multiplied numbers who did not believe or were not getting the message.

In due time, their overseas baggage arrived in Yokohama. A splendid gentleman, Mr. Yoshiki, arranged for them to live upstairs in his home. Here it was that they set up their big oil stove which they had brought from America. They also dug out of their baggage cans of milk for baby Paul. It was only a few days after being able to have this proper food that Paul was running about as if he had never been sick.

Florence, herself, started to hold Bible classes in her own home. Many people were coming to see them, particularly in the evening. As a result both Jake and Florence were holding classes for instruction. To do this, of course, meant an interpreter, for notwithstanding all the study they had made in the Japanese language in America, they were not able to converse readily in this foreign tongue. Finally, they settled down to one class between them with a very faithful Christian, helpful as the interpreter. This was Mr. Nishida, whose work during the day was being interpreter for Japanese representatives of the U. S. Military Police. After about two months, Florence had to take over all of the evening classes because Jake was out most of the time on speaking tours. Within a few weeks, five people from Mr. Yoshiki's home were baptized as Christians. Many others declared their intention of accepting Christ.

Within a few months after arriving in Japan, DeShazer had spoken in nearly two hundred different places. Since then the number has continued to grow. Because it has seemed almost impossible to get back immediately to the same place a second time, he has made it a point always to call for decisions at his very first meeting. He reports the results have been excellent:

> At nearly every place I have spoken I have asked for decisions. There has always been a large number who have responded by accepting Jesus as their Saviour. Sometimes at factories I have seen nearly every worker raise his hand indicating that he has confessed Christ now as his Lord and Saviour. Young people in the schools have shown great interest in Christianity. God is revealing the truth in Japan today after nearly two thousand years of darkness.

Under the leadership of the Holy Spirit and the light of His Word, many people who had been living lives of sin suddenly turned about face and with new courage were living Christian lives. Reports were coming to DeShazer in large numbers regarding the inspiration his messages had brought and expressing a determination to live the Christian way. The following is a sample of such letters. This was received from a young lady who indicates something of the joy she has had in her newfound experience.

> On the sixteenth of May I received new life through the message which you gave. Thank you. While you were talking I cried very much. Through your prisoner-of-war life, you have had a great deal of hatred toward the Japanese people. They were cruel in their treatment of you. I know that you have unreasonable treatment through their ignorance. I know that some Japanese are very impolite and uncultivated. Please forgive us. I have no words to apologize for our rudeness.
> However, you have forgiven us, and you came to Japan to save us. I could not help but cry to think of the love which God has put in your heart. I was a very sinful girl.

I told a lie many times, but now I have repented. I have had much trouble since becoming a Christian. Before I was a Christian, I must support my family who were in poor physical condition. I have three brothers and parents, and I had health while they were sick. I worked as a factory girl, but I was very discouraged. I tried to kill myself three or four time, but without success. I just couldn't go through with suicide. I didn't have any affection toward Japan, and I had little interest. I started working at the public welfare section as a case worker.

I always hated God, and I had contracted the sickness of heart beriberi. I quit my work but after a week I found a circular of your coming to our town to make a speech. I attended the meeting. And the sixteenth of May will always be a memorable day as well as a revolutionary day for me. By you I was reborn as a child is born on earth. I was now a child born in the heavenly kingdom. Now, "The Lord is my light and my salvation; whom shall I fear?"

Thank you very much for what you have done. I am full of hope and optimism for the future. I am learning a university course by correspondence. It will take two more years to finish this course, and then I have a hope to go and learn more of God in your country. That is only a hope, now. Please pray for me and my hope.

I hope that I can attend your next meeting near our town. Please give my kindest regards to Mrs. DeShazer and Mr. Oda. May God bless you.

DeShazer gives testimony in regard to such experiences:

It is a great joy to know that God has redeemed souls who were lost. They will rejoice throughout eternity. Glory be to God who alone is to be praised. One girl told me that her sweetheart lost his life in the raid of which I was a participant. She heard about me through pamphlets and newspaper articles, and she made up her mind that she was going to have the pleasure of taking revenge on me by killing me if it were possible. This attractive young lady came to one service which we held, and to her surprise the Spirit of Jesus showed her how wrong her intentions had been. She determined to seek this Spirit of love which Jesus gives, and God wonderfully helped her. I have seen her many times since that time, and the sweet look on her face is truly convincing of the power of Jesus to change a person's life from hatred to love. What a pleasure it is to strive for peace in this Christian way rather than to come with airplanes, bombs, and guns. How much more lasting will this Christian method of peace be than the method of war and hatred!

In the spring of 1949, nearly four years after the War's end, one of the strangest meetings that has ever happened was DeShazer's happy experience at the O. S. S. Theatre in Osaka, Japan. By pre-arrangement many of the people in Japan who had lost loved ones during the war, and as many of the Japanese guards as possible met on the platform of the big theatre with DeShazer and his wife. An unusual spirit of forgiveness seemed to pervade the entire place. DeShazer spoke to the large audience telling them about the message of forgiveness that Jesus preached nearly two thousand years ago. He told them that both they and he had been in the bitter anguish of a terrible war but that now, "We see the right thing to do is to forgive, to love one another and to work together for one another's happiness."

He told them about Jesus as God's Son and about the Holy Spirit who is able to bring light and truth. Two men, Mr. Aota and Mr. Misaka, DeShazer's prison guards, expressed their desire to become Christians. These men had been reading the Bible themselves and showing a very splendid attitude. DeShazer says:

> We are praying, not only for my former guard, but for the Spirit of Christ to spread to all of the people in Japan so that the whole nation will become a Christian nation.

CHAPTER XVII

FORTY-DAY FAST AND EXPANDING MINISTRY

Early in 1950, with impending war in Korea and continued communistic infiltration in Japan despite General MacArthur's ban on Communism, DeShazer felt a burden for further self-analysis and Spirit-anointing if his ministry was to reach the highest possible level of effectiveness. Then, too, it seemed to him that the immediate evangelism of all Japan was so imperative it could not wait for the normal operations of the various missionary boards. A miracle or a series of miracles would be necessary if Japan was to be saved from Communism on the one hand and from a cold, philosophical, and impotent Christianity on the other. Such a miracle, he felt, could come to pass only through prayer and fasting.

Thus it was that DeShazer entered upon a forty-day fast. He did not withdraw from active evangelistic work, nor did he stop his language study. During the entire period he ate practically nothing. For the first three days he went without water as well as food. After that on the advice of friends, he permitted himself to have water. He would not permit himself even to have fruit juices.

There was no thought on DeShazer's part of doing something spectacular. Rather he felt a divine urge to pray for a spiritual awakening throughout all Japan.

Many Christians as well as non-Christians were greatly impressed by DeShazer's fast. A reporter for one

Well-earned Recognition
Jake and Florence receive coveted S.P.C. "sheepskin" at hands of Pres. C. Hoyt Watson.

Off for Japan
The DeShazers wave good-bye as they leave the U. S. for missionary service in Japan.

Down the Gangplank

Arriving in Yokohama Dec. 28, 1948.

On the Dock

1. With Miss Alice Fensome.
2. With Rev. O. R. Haslam and Japanese Christians.

More Greetings

1. Col. Cyril D. Hill
2. Japanese Children.

Preaches First Sermon

Began preaching immediately with Dr. Oda as interpreter.

of the leading Japanese newspapers told Bob Pierce, of Youth for Christ, that DeShazer's fast had produced a profound effect upon the Japanese people. He suggested that DeShazer had already won the friendship of the Japanese by returning as a missionary. Now he was even fasting for them! They had been accustomed to the fastings of the Buddhist priests but seldom or never had they known of a foreign missionary fasting. The reporter further stated that there were many things about Christianity they could not understand, but that they could understand DeShazer, and they liked him.

Within a week after the termination of his fast, seven different Christian ministers called on DeShazer to inquire regarding fasting as a Christian activity. Evidently they, too, had a heart hunger for more of God.

DeShazer reports that his fasting was a very rewarding experience. From that time on God has been answering his prayer. One of the first evidences was the conversion on April 14, 1950, of Mitsuo Fuchida, Commander of the three hundred sixty planes of the Japanese air squadron which bombed Pearl Harbor on that fateful December 7, 1941. His conversion was a tangible demonstration of God's miracle-working power. Fuchida has written the wonderful story of his conversion in tract form which has been distributed widely by the Pocket Testament League.

This tract tells about the unique manner in which God used DeShazer's testimony "I Was a Prisoner of Japan" (a tract published by the Bible Meditation League) to bring Fuchida under conviction. Within a month after his conversion, he had the privilege of being with DeShazer in a great mass meeting in the largest auditorium in Osaka, where both men gave their testimonies. At least 4,000 people had been crowded into the auditorium and as many as 3,000 were outside unable to enter. At the close of the meeting approximately 500 individuals came down the aisles as seekers for the Christian way of life.

Further evidences of God's leadership and blessing continued in DeShazer's life day after day. But he was not alone in this regard. This same spirit of aggressiveness was also gripping other missionaries in Japan and through them reaching back to their sponsoring missionary boards. There was, and still is, a general feeling that every Christian should be active and alert along missionary lines. It is admitted that God, of course, will use every available and consecrated person. At the same time it is also admitted that the real revival which Japan needs can come about only through the miracle work of God, in answer to prayer.

It is well known that when the United Nations' Army, spearheaded by the United States of America, went into Korea it was the signal for an all-out conflict between the forces of Democracy and Communism. With the infiltration of followers of Karl Marx into governmental positions in the United States and the over-run of many countries in Europe and the Orient with Red propaganda grave doubts have been entertained by many regarding the possibility of America and the United Nations winning such a conflict. In any event, Christian statesmen throughout the world realize, in the military conflict as well as in the conflict of ideas resulting from such an all-out effort, that Japan because of its strategic location will inevitably be at the crossroads. This accounts in large measure for the increased missionary interest now being shown by many missionary boards and particularly those which are evangelical. The response to the great opportunity has been phenomenal.

At the close of the Second World War, missionary activity had been going on in Japan for approximately ninety-five years. Much good work had been done. At the same time the progress actually made by Christian missions was pitifully slow and the successes disappointingly small. Here was a pagan nation, well-trained, highly intellectual, proud, and, before the War, powerful. Many leaders think the Japanese people were and perhaps still are the natural leaders of the Orient. They had tolerated Christian missionaries but seldom had given encouragement. Then came the War and with it military and political defeat. But fortunately for the Japanese, with cessation of hostilities also came General MacArthur.

When General MacArthur took over, the situation for Christian work in Japan was changed completely. Due very largely to his vision and statesmanship the way was quickly opened for the evangelization of Japan's 81,500,-000 people. All the missionary societies of Christendom rejoiced and attempted to swing into action. Stories of great sacrifice and miracles similar to DeShazer's aroused further interest and increased the effort.

As a result, every missionary and every mission board began to feel the need for immediate action. In fact, the entire Christian world came to feel that within a very few years the die would be cast with respect to the future of Japan. A casual glance at the titles of magazine articles and books then appearing indicates something of the widespread interest in the outcome of Christian missions in Japan.

Here are a few of such titles : "Japan—Hotspot of Missions," "Advance to the Villages," "Japan Can be a Christian Nation," "Keep the Bibles Rolling," "Make it Ten Million," "Opportunity to Win a Nation," "God's Day for Japan," "Communism or Christ in Japan," "Japan Will be Saved," "Today, the Door Is Open," "Christ for all Japan," "Christianity Advancing in Japan," "Which Way Japan?" and "Pentecost in Japan."

It became apparent when the missions began responding to the new opportunity that they could no longer limit themselves to a single type of missionary service. Open doors were everywhere. This explains why a given missionary agency, for instance, which originally had in mind only the distribution of Christian literature found it necessary to expand its services. This was most commendable.

To give a better perspective of the various forces making for evangelization in Japan it will be helpful to describe some of the essential activities now being carried out by the several missions and missionary agencies. These essential activities will be presented under five headings—Evangelism, Literature, Radio, Education and Missionaries.

Evangelism. Perhaps the most significant missionary activity now going on in Japan is that of evangelism. This includes both the mass evangelistic meetings in the great city centers and also rural evangelism. Three of the agencies which are doing effective work in the field of mass evangelism are The Free Methodist Missions, The Pocket Testament League, and The Youth for Christ.

DeShazer is being used by all three of these agencies and also by the Japanese Christian Church. The Pocket Testament League under the leadership of its Foreign Secretary, Glen Wagner, has sponsored many mass meetings, some of them reaching 8,000 or more in attendance. Such was the case at Nagoya, where at least 700 responded to the call for public confessions of Christ. The Youth for Christ mass meetings have also brought together many thousands under the leadership of such men as David Morken, Fred Jarvis, and Bob Pierce. Responses in these meetings also number in the hundreds.

In addition to t h e s e leading agencies for mass evangelism are many individual missionaries who have been holding open-air and street meetings.

Careful observers of developments in Japan with respect to mass meetings are agreed upon two conclusions. First, it is very obvious the holding of such meetings is becoming increasingly difficult. Apparently, merely to announce a meeting does not grip the popular Japanese mind as much as it did earlier. Second, it is also agreed that the large number reported as seekers in these mass meetings is not a true index of the number who have experienced bona fide conversions. DeShazer and other speakers in evangelistic services state that the effectiveness of the decisions and their permanency depend very largely upon the follow-up on the part of Christian workers after the meetings. Unfortunately this follow-up has been weak.

In connection with rural evangelism at least four different agencies are very active. These are The Far Eastern Gospel Crusade, The Oriental Missionary Society, The Japan Evangelistic Band, and The Evangelical Alliance Mission. The fact that 67% of the population of Japan live in rural areas or in towns and villages with less than ten thousand population makes it obvious that the complete evangelization of Japan must of necessity include much emphasis upon rural evangelism.

The Far Eastern Gospel Crusade now has many missionaries in the so-called back country. Rev. Philip E. Armstrong is the executive secretary and Rev. Leonard E. Sweet is field chairman of the Japanese missionaries. The Oriental Missionary Society is circularizing whole villages with tracts through house-to-house distribution. The Japan Evangelistic Band is holding many tent meetings in villages. The Evangelical Alliance Mission and still other missions and missionaries are also doing significant rural work.

Literature. A second phase of the total missionary activity being carried on in Japan today has to do with the printing and distribution of Christian literature. The need for such literature in Japan has been rather highly advertised. The full import of the need, however, has not been fully understood.

The Far Eastern Gospel Crusade made a survey of some 1,000 Japanese books and pamphlets having to do with the Bible, Christian life and doctrine and the plan of Salvation. They found that only about thirty of these could be given unqualified recommendation as being evangelical. Between fifty and one hundred others received their recommendation but with reservations. Obviously, the need for more Christian literature is imperative. Much effort is being put forth to meet this need.

The Pocket Testament League has already distributed five million copies of the Gospel of John. The League hopes to put out at least five million more within a year. It has distributed 300,000 special copies of the New Testament. All of these materials were printed in Japan.

The Plymouth Brethren have put out several tracts for children and adults. The Worldwide Evangelistic Crusade has launched a very comprehensive literature crusade. The Gideons are distributing Testaments. Other agencies are planning to make reprints of good Christian books.

The Bible Meditation League under its president, Dr. Don R. Falkenberg, has distributed more than two million copies of the DeShazer tract "I Was a Prisoner of Japan." This tract probably has had greater influence in Japan in the present evangelistic movement than any other piece of literature save the Gospel of John. Under the leadership of the League at least ten thousand people in Japan are reported now to be studying the Bible by correspondence.

The Youth for Christ is cooperating with The Pocket Testament League and with The Inter-Varsity Christian Fellowship in the distribution of tracts on "How to Grow in Grace." The Japan Bible Society has published and sold at least four and one half million copies of the Bible or portions of the Bible since the war. It is assisted in this work by a subsidy from The American Bible Society. The *Jordan Press* (Southern Baptist), The Oriental Missionary Society and The Reformed Japanese Presbyterian Church, among others are putting out Gospel tracts and other printed literature.

Radio. Many who sense the urgency of the situation in Japan with respect to acting quickly for the immediate evangelization of the entire country have a vision of a radio network to blanket all of Japan. This is the third over-all type of activity, at least potentially speaking, for advancing the Gospel. Fifteen evangelical mission groups have formed an organization known as the Evangelical Missions Association of Japan. This Association has sponsored the Japan Christian Broadcasting Corporation. Under this corporate name they have applied to the Japanese authorities for an independent radio network. There are grave doubts whether this will be granted. Indeed, many missionaries feel that to have an independent radio network may not be the best plan. It is understood that if the proposed plan fails, the evangelical mission groups will then buy blocks of time on existing networks.

It is common knowledge that the Catholics of Japan have also made request to the Japanese authorities for permission to operate a radio network. In their case, however, favorable action seems to have been assured for they are already constructing their radio building. It is expected that their network will consist of eleven stations.

There are many hurdles to overcome before the Protestant missions can carry on the radio program desired. One of these is the practical problem of many missionary boards working together.

It is quite agreed that it would be unwise for the separate missions to carry on independent radio programs. Protestant churches in America, unfortunately, have not developed a satisfactory technique and procedure for this type of cooperative endeavor. To the credit of missionaries it should be said that there is a far greater spirit of cooperation on the mission field than in the homeland.

It is agreed that the present hour in Japan presents to Protestantism something more than a splendid opportunity. It is a "must." Action is imperative. Radio can be the material means of reaching multiplied millions with the Gospel message. But radio evangelism, in Japan like anywhere else, requires consecrated leadership, material equipment, and technically trained men and women. Once again, here is cause for the Christian

DeShazer Shakes Hands with Former Guard
This former guard came to hear DeShazer speak. He became interested in Christian message.

DeShazer Has Many Speaking Engagements

1. In a Department Store.
2. At a Buddhist School.

1. She had vowed she would kill DeShazer
2. A Street Meeting.

Preaches at Suginami
Recently rebuilt Free Methodist Church.

Many Outdoor Meetings
DeShazer with Oda preaching before
bomb shattered monument.

Love Always Wins
People of Nagoya who shot at DeShazer when he dropped bombs on them
present him with bouquet of flowers.

church to go to its knees in intercessory prayer. Certainly the Lord has a solution to the problem.

Education. A fourth area of activity which is now receiving much time and thought on the part of missionaries and workers in Japan is that of education.

Prior to the War much of the Christian educational work in Japan was like much so-called Christian education in America—it was largely Christian in name only. In many mission-sponsored schools, colleges, and universities, the emphasis was largely intellectual with only conventional attention being given to spiritual life and activity.

When the war ended and opportunity for accelerated action suddenly came to all missionary agencies in Japan, the missionary boards were quick to see their obligation to open and maintain Christian schools. In the first place there was a call for Bible schools which could quickly train Japanese men and women to do personal evangelism, lead Bible study groups, teach Sunday-school classes, witness in public, and preach. It was perfectly clear that the evangelization of Japan could not be carried out by missionaries alone. Native workers by the hundreds and, if possible, by the thousands must be trained.

In addition to training schools for adult Christian workers was the longer range planning for the Christian education of the youth of Japan. The Japanese people for many years have been strong for education. In the years since the War they have placed further emphasis upon schooling.

Particularly appealing is the study of English. Because of this the missionaries are being bombarded daily with calls to come to local schools, industrial plants, and business organizations to teach English. If the missionaries were to accept such invitations, they could spend their entire time merely teaching English. In spite of the new emphasis on education, the fact still remains that most of the middle and higher education in Japan is dominated by ancient Japanese philosophy or is a mixture of such philosophy and liberalism. There is little place in most of these schools—even with Christian missionary traditions—for evangelical truth. Many Christian leaders are greatly concerned over the apparent influence, if not actual control, of postwar higher education in Japan by liberals in both religion and government. General MacArthur's educational leaders unfortunately are not following him in his emphasis upon spiritual values.

The picture is rather dark. Prior to the War the evangelical missions gave practically no attention to higher education or graduate theological studies. One notable exception was the theological seminary in Osaka maintained by the Free Methodist Missionary Board. This school was completely destroyed by bombs during the War. It has now been partially reconstructed and is functioning largely as a collegiate institution rather than as a seminary. Although its enrollment is small, it is stated by unbiased reporters to be one of the best postwar evangelical institutions for higher education in Japan.

Some effort has been put forth to get several evangelical missions to work together in promoting a Bible institute or a Christian college, rather than each one aspire to operate a school. The progress along this line, though small, is indicative of what could be done through cooperative endeavor. It must be stated, however, that as yet (five years after the war) not a single new evangelical school has an enrollment as high as thirty. Much remains to be done in this area.

Groups doing sacrificial work along one or more lines of Bible training or regular high school or college work include The Free Methodist Missionary Board, The Japan Evangelistic Band, The Far Eastern Gospel Crusade, The Oriental Missionary Society, The Reformed Church, The Wesleyan Methodist Missionary Board, and The Conservative Baptist Missionary Board.

Some organizations, rather than sponsor schools themselves, are giving attention in an effort to evangelize the students attending the long established schools, colleges, and universities. In this connection, good is being done by the Inter-Varsity Christian Fellowship whose leaders visit the college and university campuses and work with students in organizing Bible study groups and in giving guidance in various forms of personal and evangelistic work. Other groups also promoting this type of work include the Japan Evangelistic Band, the Evangelical Alliance Mission, the Conservative Baptist Mission, the Youth for Christ, and the Pocket Testament League.

Missionaries. The fifth area of consideration regarding over-all activity at the present time on the part of Missions in Japan has to do with the missionaries themselves —or what may be called direct missionary work. Let us look at the present status of missionary personnel in Japan.

From one point of view the most important organization in Japan today is the Evangelical Missionary Association of Japan. This is not an organization of missions or of missionary boards but rather an organization of missionaries themselves. It includes in its membership representatives of at least sixteen different evangelical groups. The Reverend Donald E. Hoke, assistant to the president of Columbia Bible College and a special editor of *The Christian Life Magazine,* reported upon his return from a five-month assignment in Japan that there are approximately 900 recognized Protestant missionaries in Japan. According to his investigation and evaluation, approximately half of this number could be considered evangelical. There are approximately 700 Catholic missionaries. Of course there are still other missionaries from various schismatic groups such as the Mormans. The bulk of the missionaries are from America.

Much publicity has been given to General Mac-Arthur's statement of needing additional missionaries. This is true. At the same time, there is of necessity a very definite lag between the time some one in America consecrates his life to do missionary work in Japan and the time when such individual arrives and can carry out effective missionary work. In other words the period required for training and for language study and also to get acquainted with the Oriental background means that there will be many months and perhaps years before the Christian church of America and England can make a large contribution of people to go to Japan to do direct missionary work.

This is highly appropriate for a long range program. It is connected definitely with the educational program and the training and influencing of children and youth of Japan. The grave need during the next few years, however, is believed to include an all out commitment of the Christian church in prayer in behalf of a God-inspired and God-ordained revival throughout Japan. If the power of God in answer to prayer is released, an unprecedented revival can sweep Japan which would be more effective than perhaps a hundred years of devoted service by many missionaries.

Such is the picture today as DeShazer continues to preach the Gospel. It would be easy for him to let up until the Christian people of America "prayed down" a revival for Japan. But no, he is giving himself without stint.

Soon after the conversion of Fuchida, DeShazer with his chief interpreter, the Reverend Dr. Kaneo Oda, began extensive evangelistic tours. They spent a month or more with the coal miners on Kyushu Island. Here they held two meetings a day with an average attendance of 1000 or more. Opportunity was given for those interested to remain after each service for prayer. Many thus remained, the number in several instances reaching as high as 400. From Kyushu they went to Hiroshima, the city of the atom bomb, for a series of meetings.

As this printed biographical story concludes, DeShazer and Oda with a Gospel Sound Truck are making a tour of the coal mines of Hokkaido. With the mounted public-address system they are holding many street meetings. Gospel literature in large quantities is being distributed. God is blessing in a most gracious way. The work and the marvelous life of DeShazer goes forward!